UNITY LIBRARY 8 ARCHIVES
Living with others: guide book

W9-CZU-140

DATE DUE

Guidebook for Leaders in Junior Camps

$\mathcal{L}$IVING WITH OTHERS

CARRIE LOU GODDARD

in Cooperation with the Special Committee on Camps and Conferences, Division of Christian Education, National Council of the Churches of Christ in the U.S.A.

ILLUSTRATIONS BY EDWIN N. GODDARD

UNITY SCHOOL LIBRARY
Unity Village
Lee's Summit, Missouri 64063

PUBLISHED FOR

The Cooperative Publication Association

BY

ABINGDON PRESS

NEW YORK • NASHVILLE

LIVING WITH OTHERS

Copyright © MCMLIX by Abingdon Press

All rights in this book are reserved.
No part of the book may be reproduced in any
manner whatsoever without written permission of
the publishers except brief quotations embodied in
critical articles or reviews. For information address
Abingdon Press, Nashville 2, Tennessee.

Library of Congress Catalog Card Number: 59-5544

Scripture quotations, unless otherwise noted, are from the Revised Standard Version
of the Bible and are copyrighted 1946, 1952 by Division of Christian Education of
the National Council of the Churches of Christ in the United States of America.

The Cooperative Series

The camping program of the Protestant churches requires curricular materials of
high order. To secure such materials the thirty-nine Protestant denominations in the
Division of Christian Education of the National Council of the Churches of Christ in
the U.S.A. have established the Cooperative Publication Association. This agency is
an interdenominational group of denominational editors and publishers which selects
the writers and provides editorial supervision to insure sound educational values,
practical usefulness and interdenominational approval and acceptance. *Living with
Others* is part of this program prepared for juniors and has the approval of the Special
Committee on Camps and Conferences.

SET UP, PRINTED, AND BOUND BY THE
PARTHENON PRESS, AT NASHVILLE,
TENNESSEE, UNITED STATES OF AMERICA

Contents

Meet David

David sat on the edge of the car seat and watched the changing scenery outside the window. It was July and David was on his way to camp. It had been fun getting his clothes and bedding ready for the days at camp. Occasionally he ran his fingers over the new knife in his pocket and wondered if there would be an opportunity for using it. He checked the sheathed ax lying on the floor at his feet. Everything was fine. He looked at the road again. He wondered what camp would be like.

Suddenly the car turned off the main highway and bumped along a side road. "This must be it," David thought as he watched the clouds of dust rising behind the car.

"Well, here we are," Dad said as he opened the car door and stepped out.

David got out of the car and looked around. His eager eyes saw the lake first. There were the diving board and the raft. David's eyes lighted up when he saw the boats tied at the wharf. He liked the water.

On the way to the long shed David stopped to look at a clump of gray birches. Nearby was a pile of rocks. They looked as if they had been there a long time. Some were covered with moss and lichens. "Good place for snakes," David thought. He began to poke around to see if he could find one.

"David, David," he heard Dad calling. "Come on and meet your group."

When David arrived at the long shed he saw Dad talking to a tall

blond man. Dad called him Ray. David liked the way Ray looked. He was stretching up to see what Ray had in his hand when Dad said, "David, this is Ray. He will be one of your counselors."

Ray smiled and stretched out his hand. David felt quite grown-up as he shook hands with Ray. He had seen his dad shake hands with his friends. "David, I am making a name tag," Ray said, holding the piece of cedar wood so David could see it. "Feel how smooth the top is getting. There is more wood here if you would like a piece, too."

"Come over here, fellows," Ray called to a group of boys standing to one side. When the boys came closer Ray said, "This is David. He is the last member of our group to arrive. David, these are the boys you will know and work with here at camp."

David looked at each one of them. He did not feel too comfortable with so many new faces all at once. Then he saw that each boy was working on a piece of wood just as Ray had been. Ray was holding some extra pieces for him to choose one of his own.

"Here is some sandpaper," Tom said, pulling a piece from his hip pocket. "Rub your wood like this."

David took the sandpaper and began to rub as Tom had showed him. He liked the sound of the sandpaper against the wood. He liked the spicy smell of the cedar as he sanded.

The boys sanded the pieces of cedar wood as they walked along the path with Ray. He led them along the water front to a shaded spot. The boys sat with Ray on some big gray rocks.

"We will wait here for the girls," Ray said.

"Girls!" the boys said in surprise. "Are there going to be girls with us?"

"Sure," Ray said, "why not?"

"Aw, I don't like girls," Tom said in disgust.

"We will need their help before camp is over," Ray said. "Here they come now."

David saw the girls coming across the meadow. Their counselor was with them. They were playing with some tall meadow grasses they had gathered on the way. When they came closer Ray smiled and said, "Fellows, this is Betty, another counselor, with the other members of our group."

"Girls!" David said in disgust. "I don't like girls!"

"I am sorry you don't like girls," Betty said. David thought she had the friendliest smile he had ever seen. "I like you, David," Betty said.

David looked at her for a moment in surprise. "Well," he said lamely, "but you are different."

"Let's all sit here on the rocks," Betty said, "and plan what we want to do at camp." The boys all gathered around Ray. The girls sat with Betty.

Ray began to sing. David liked the gay melody. He wished he knew the words. David grinned when Ray started the next song. He knew that one! After several songs David began to feel more comfortable in the group. It was fun to sing together.

"Since we are going to be spending several days together at camp," Betty said after they had sung awhile, "we need to think about what we want to do."

"Cook out!" Tom said promptly.

"Go boating," came another voice.

"Learn to swim."

"Hike."

The answers came thick and fast. David thought about his knife. He felt to see if it was still in his pocket. He wondered if he dared mention that he wanted to use his knife at camp. He looked across at Ray. Ray was smiling at him. Ray seemed to understand.

"I hope you all have knives," Ray said. "We will need them for several of the activities you have said you want to do at camp."

"And with this long list of things to be done," Betty added, "we had better get to work. First of all we will need a camp site where we can cook. We need to set a time for swimming and boating. We will need to plan for our hikes, where we want to go and when. Where shall we begin?"

There was a whole chorus of voices then. David did not really know who was saying what. He saw Ray hold up his hand for silence.

"Everyone wants to begin with the activity he has chosen," Ray said with a smile. "Let's make out a work schedule. Then everyone will get to do the activity he has chosen before we leave camp."

Betty wrote the schedule on a piece of notebook paper as the group worked it out. David was glad when they decided to go out in the boats just after they went swimming. "We can wear our swim suits and won't have to change but once," Betty said.

"We can work on our camp site before swim time," Ray added. "Just about time we get hot and tired it will be time to swim."

"Let's get to work," Tom said. "I'm tired of talking."

"A very good idea, Tom," Betty said. "I am glad we have a camp and so many exciting things to do."

Ray looked quietly around the group. "I'm glad, too," he said. "Before we go I want to thank God for this chance to live and work together at camp."

There was a moment of quiet before Ray's voice began to pray. David could hear the waves slapping against the shore. A wood's peewee was calling lazily from a nearby pine tree. Ray's voice was quiet and reverent.

"Thank you, God," Ray prayed, "for all the interesting and wonderful things in this world around us. We are glad to be at camp. We are glad

7

for all the exciting activities we have chosen to do. Help us to work together happily and co-operatively so they will all get done. Amen."

After the prayer Ray led the way down the path toward the woods. "Everyone watch for a good camp site," he called.

David followed along the path. He felt glad and happy inside. He was a bit excited, too. He began to wonder how they would build a camp site after they found the place. "Ray will know," he thought. "He will help us."

BEFORE DAVID ARRIVED AT CAMP

David's beginning at camp seemed smooth and even and it was. However, much planning, work and study had gone into making it so. Let us move behind the scene of his arrival at camp and discover some of the reasons why his beginning was smooth and comfortable and pleasant.

A CAMP COMMITTEE
Somewhere behind David's arrival at camp was a committee. It may have been a few people from the local church if only one church was involved in this camp experience for junior boys and girls. It may have been made up of representatives from several churches if this was a community or larger area camp enterprise. Whether this was a local church, a community or a larger area camp the members of the planning committee had several characteristics in common. These characteristics were:

1. A vital Christian experience of their own.

2. Some knowledge of the Christian education of children and of the church's program for them.

3. A genuine love for and understanding of junior boys and girls.

4. An enjoyment of camping and an understanding of the contribution it can make to Christian growth.

This committee had probably been at work at least a year before David got to camp. Sometimes it is necessary for a committee to work more than a year before bringing juniors to camp. Here are a few of the things that must be done:

I. SECURE A CAMP SITE
Whether it is a day camp or a resident camp there must be a site! What are the basic essentials of a good site? Here are some:

1. *Outdoor space*—as much as possible and as interesting and varied as can be! Such a spacious site allows for explorations, discoveries, and

experimentation; provides varied experiences in meadowland, along the water, through the woodland, and gives opportunity for several groups to work without interfering with each other.

2. *Shelter.* Day campers need shelter for books, for equipment, and for personal belongings. Then, of course, there is always the possibility of rain and the need for a place to dry out or to relax with crafts and other rainy day activities. Resident campers need, in addition to this, a place for sleeping and for personal belongings in larger quantities than those of a day camper. Also it is important for resident campers to have the security and comfort at bedtime of a small group with an adult counselor.

3. *Safe water supply.* Water is one of the essentials of life. Any camp must make provision for safe drinking water. There are other uses for water that must be considered, too. These may include handwashing, cooking, bathing, and craft work.

II. Secure a Staff

The staff sets the tone of the camp. If the camp atmosphere is to be one of freedom, of joy, of wholesome Christian co-operation these attitudes must be characteristic of each member of the staff. If there is to be a deep undergirding of those spiritual qualities that make life truly Christian those qualities must be in the lives of those who set the tone. If junior boys and girls are going to feel understood, loved and helped by the experience at camp the staff must be one that can provide those feelings.

All of this does not mean that the staff must be perfect for such a one does not exist. But it is saying that these qualities must be present in as strong a degree as possible in each member of the staff.

How many people are needed on a camp staff? Who are the essential ones? The following paragraphs describe those considered most essential.

Director. Someone must take responsibility for guiding the organization, helping to plan the program and for the general atmosphere of the camp. This is the director.

The director has the responsibility of working with both the adult and junior campers. He must be able to help the small group leaders plan and work with each other as well as with boys and girls. His philosophy of life and his own personality will do much to create the atmosphere of the camp. An ability to understand situations and persons, to sympathize, to adjust to sudden changes and to give a feeling of acceptance and security are very important qualifications of a director. These characteristics will help as he works both with the adults and with the juniors in camp.

The more the director understands and knows junior boys and girls, the greater his knowledge of the Christian philosophy and the skills of camping, and the stronger his ability to work with groups and individuals, the more he will bring to the camp. It follows then that camping will be a much happier and much more worthwhile experience for all involved.

The Counselors or Small Group Leaders. These are the persons who work most closely with the boys and girls. Each small group should have a Ray and a Betty, a man with the boys and a woman with the girls. Not that the lines between boys and girls are sharply drawn, but each group must have someone who understands their needs and to whom they can come for counsel and comfort. An illustration of such a need was a junior girl's emergency need to go to the toilet while on a hike. It was the woman counselor who understood and helped to solve the problem.

Junior children need fellowship with Christian men and women. One of the developmental tasks of this age group is that of defining their sex roles and identifying themselves with their own sex role. Loving, understanding, mature counselors can help junior boys and girls define and identify themselves with their sex roles. This is most easily accomplished when boys and girls live in happy wholesome fellowship with mature counselors who exemplify Christian womanhood and manhood. Christian ways of thinking and acting, Christian attitudes toward others and toward self are absorbed rather than taught in such surroundings.

Much self-giving is required of small group leaders. They give of their physical strength and energy, they give of their time and patience, they give of themselves, but there is no greater reward than theirs! To help boys and girls find their place in a group, knowing that this will also help them find their place in life; to see them grow in knowledge and understanding of the universe and man's place in it; and to have fellowship with them in a Christian relationship is a very high and holy privilege.

Other Staff Members. Some arrangements must be made for emergencies and caring for physical needs. It is not necessary to have a doctor on the camp grounds but one should be available in case of emergency. It is very comforting to have a nurse or first-aider close by for small needs such as insect stings and scratches as well as for the larger needs of a

knife cut or a bad bruise. A person who is trained as a first-aider takes these responsibilities in a day camp. A resident camp must have a nurse on the staff. In case of emergency, such as a broken bone, it is the nurse who can take over with assurance until the doctor arrives or is reached.

If swimming and boating are included in the program, they must be supervised. Unless the counselors are certified lifeguards and capable of assuming this responsibility an extra staff person will be needed. The water front director should be part of the fellowship of the camp staff and should be aware of his place in helping to nurture the Christian growth of each camper.

Other staff members are determined by the kind of camp and the local situation. There may be a business manager, a registrar and, in resident camps, a dietitian and staff of cooks. In so far as possible, these persons should participate in the staff fellowship, know the objectives of the camp, and share in the joys of the camp activities.

If we are truly concerned about junior boys and girls there can be no shortcuts because of finances or because of the difficulty of finding the necessary personnel. A Christian concern for personality forces us to leave no stone unturned to care properly for every camper.

III. Train the Staff

How did Ray and Betty know about the rocks beside the lake as a place of meeting for their group? Why did their guidance of the group flow so smoothly back and forth between the two of them? It did not just happen that way.

First of all, both Ray and Betty knew something about the philosophy underlying Christian camping. They not only knew something of this philosophy but accepted it. Thus they committed themselves to work wholeheartedly toward its goals.

Second, during the pre-camp training Ray and Betty had been over the grounds of the camp. They had walked along the lake, sat on the rocks, climbed the hills, investigated, enjoyed, and learned on their own. They already had interesting knowledge and experience which had been gained on this spot to share with this group. They were at home in this particular area of God's world and were ready to open its doors to others.

Third, there had been time for the two of them to plan for these days in camp. They had discussed and listed in their notebooks the many possibilities of what might be done. They had helped each other to grow in certain camp skills that might be needed. They had recognized the areas in which each might make his own best contribution. For instance, Ray should probably take leadership in most of the singing. Betty might do a better job of storytelling. This recognition served later as a good basis for co-operative leadership.

Secure in the concept that their most important contribution would be to live with these boys and girls in a Christian fellowship they were ready to open the door wide and say, "What do you want to do?" Their time of thinking together and of practicing skills gave to each a feeling of security in the other. Had they been asked they might have said, "If neither of us knows how, maybe we can work it out together. If we fail to find a solution we have had the experience of working together and of accepting our limitations." These are important learnings and learnings that children need and can absorb from counselors.

The opportunity for such growth on the part of Ray and Betty was provided for in the pre-camp training by the camp committee. Ray and Betty had spent time with the other staff members at the camp site. The staff had talked about the philosophy of camping and had come to a common understanding of it. They had cooked an outdoor meal together, had explored on the site, and had planned together. A rich fellowship was already created before children were brought into it.

IV. REGISTER THE CHILDREN

David was introduced to Ray by his Dad. Ray was expecting David and knew that he had a new knife for camp. Information sheets provided the director of the camp with enough background about David to know that he would be happy with Ray. Ray learned about the knife David had received for his birthday from the same source.

An accurate registration of children and information sheets that have been carefully phrased can make relationships easy from the beginning moments of camp. Both counselor and camper are made to feel secure and at ease and camp is off to a good start!

FOR MORE SPECIFIC HELP

The suggestions with regard to organization and administration given on these pages are far from adequate. Specific help for camp committees, directors, and small group leaders may be found in the two books *The Church Day Camp* and *Planning the Church Camp* by LaDonna Bogardus.

2

David uses the ax

There was a busy hum from the pine thicket on top of the hill. There were the buzzing of saws, the snap and crackle of dead limbs, and the sound of happy voices.

David's group had chosen this knoll in the midst of the pine thicket for their camp site. No group had camped on the knoll and there was much to be done to make it into a good camp site. The ground had to be cleared of dead branches, tables had to be lashed, a fireplace built, tarpaulin put up for shelter, and latrines dug. Everyone had chosen a job and even Ray and Betty were at work.

David unsheathed his ax and watched carefully as Ray showed him how to use it safely. Then he began to look for a sapling the right size for making the table. Ray showed him how to choose the spindling ones that were shaded by the tall pines. "They will hinder the growth of those around them. It is good woodsmanship to cut out such saplings. We can use them in lashing the table."

Tom and Cavin practiced using the saw on some of the dead limbs that had fallen to the ground. They had chosen the job of cutting the saplings into the proper lengths for the table that was to be lashed between two tall pine trees. David was glad he knew how to use an ax. He liked chopping better than sawing.

Mirian and Carol were working with Betty getting ready to lash the table. Each girl cut a long piece of twine. Betty showed them how to tie a strong knot and how to hold the twine tight so that the table would be secure.

The first sapling fell and Tom marked the lengths with his measuring

13

stick. Cavin began to saw. "This is quite a production line," Betty said with a grin. "Each one has his work to do and with everyone working a table is made."

After the second sapling was cut David paused for a moment to watch Mirian and Carol at work on the table. Their lashing was neat and even.

"Hey! That's pretty keen," he said admiringly.

"It is a good strong table," Betty said. "It will hold our food when we cook out. The girls are doing a good job with an under and over lashing."

"You better get back to work," Tom called. "We're almost ready for another sapling."

David looked around. It was getting easier for him to choose the saplings to be cut. He remembered what Ray had said about finding those that got little or no sun and were crowded with other trees.

Over in the clearing Ray and the other boys were cleaning out a place for the fire. Some of the girls helped by carrying the dead limbs and brush away from camp.

David could hardly believe his ears when he heard Ray calling, "Time for a swim!" Everyone dropped what he was doing and started to run.

"Whoa!" Ray called with a grin. "Not quite so fast! Where are your tools? They must be cared for before we go."

The shovels, saws, and axes were carefully put away so no one would stumble over them and be hurt. Knives were closed and stored away in pockets. Ray looked around. "Neat and orderly," he said. "That is the way to leave a camp site. That is the mark of a good camper."

"Since no one goes swimming until everyone is ready we will save time by traveling together," Ray said as he started down the trail. David took a last look to see that his ax was safely put away. He and Betty were the last to leave the knoll.

"David, you certainly handle an ax well," Betty said as they walked along together.

David looked at her for a moment. "Thank you for the compliment," he said. Then he added, "You're doing a good job, too."

David was thoughtful as he walked on down the hill toward the lake. He was thinking about the neat table Mirian and Carol were making. He remembered the help the other girls had given in clearing the camp site. Maybe girls weren't so bad after all!

14

A PROGRAM FOR DAVID
WHILE IN CAMP

Anyone visiting the knoll in the pine thicket after the group had gone swimming would have sensed immediately the loneliness and emptiness of the place. It is quite apparent in such a circumstance that it is people —boys and girls, counselors and campers—who are vital to the camp. It exists because of them and for them. As they live and work together at the common tasks they have set for themselves, the interdependence of human beings, the interrelatedness of life itself, and the joy of human fellowship are experienced. The commandment, "Love your neighbor," has new depths of meaning for both small group leader and camper. "In the beginning God . . ." has new significance as campers come closer to the Creator in the wonderful world he has brought into being.

WHAT IS THE PROGRAM?

A casual observer on the knoll in the pine thicket might have said that the program was learning to lash a table, to use a saw or to build a fireplace. A little more careful observer might have added that good woodsmanship and good camping habits were also being learned. A still keener observer would have been aware that all those activities were but means to ends. They were but the living situations in which boys and girls were confronted with problems of relating themselves to each other and to their world. In this living relationship the spiritual qualities of human fellowship were experienced, evaluated, and accepted or rejected.

Ray and Betty were helping to create an environment where appreciations could grow: appreciation for God's creative processes, appreciation for each other, and appreciation for one's own self. They were helping to create an environment where Christian attitudes and habits could be experienced and evaluated. Their own relationship to each other and to the campers said, "This is a way of life that is good, it is happy, it is the Christian way." Thus the program or curriculum of camp essentially becomes the campers themselves. It is their growth in Christian appreciations, ways of thinking and acting, and ability to live together in a Christian community that is of utmost importance.

Camp is only one of the many channels for helping boys and girls grow in the Christian way of life but, because its experiences are new to most of them and its relationships different, it can be both challenging and effective. If the junior camp is to accomplish its purpose counselors must be aware of the particular contribution it has to make, must be able to use its skills, and must know and understand the boys and girls who make its program.

15

Wholesome acceptance and appreciation of the boys for the girls, the ability to accept and carry through individual as well as group responsibilities, and to achieve the satisfactions of happy group life were recognized in the opening session as problems for which Ray and Betty should provide some help. Other problems evolved as the days went by but these were apparent from the beginning. Betty and Ray did not argue or try to force co-operation between boys and girls. Activities were set up that made co-operation between boys and girls a natural working situation in order to accomplish the goals they had set for themselves. Smaller committees, each working on a necessary part of the camp site, provided opportunities for accepting and carrying through individual and group responsibilities. Each camper was given a task that was within his ability to achieve. Ray's and Betty's obvious enjoyment of the outdoors, of the camp activities and of the boys and girls themselves created a pleasant and happy atmosphere.

What is the program? It is the campers themselves, skillfully placed by understanding counselors into living situations where they can grow in Christian ways.

THE BOYS AND GIRLS

A small group leader would find it much easier to live and work with his group in camp if he could turn to a list of characteristics of children this age and know, "This is what the junior child is like." However, that is an impossibility, for no two of these junior boys and girls are alike. Their differences are due to native inheritance and environment. Even children in the same family inherit such varying traits and are often so different that one wonders how they could belong to the same parents.

As each personality lives in and responds to an environment, learning takes place. Here again no two people have exactly the same environment and therefore do not have exactly the same learnings. Each individual has his own peculiar problems of living in his particular environment. His total growth pattern is affected by the pressures exerted upon him in his environment and the responses he makes to them.

16

A third strong influence upon a child's growth and development are those special problems he must solve and the adjustments he must make to the people and world about him. Biological maturation creates the problems and the resulting inner pressures. The expectancies of the culture in which he lives determine the adjustments he must make. These problems and the adjustments that must be made come in a definite pattern and at about the same stage of development for all children. These are therefore called developmental tasks.

Some knowledge of these problems and the adjustments that needed to be made helped Ray and Betty to provide encouragement and guidance for each member of their group. It gave them wisdom for arranging opportunities that would facilitate the achieving, in part at least, of these tasks. Here is the list of developmental tasks of middle childhood that Betty and Ray studied before going to camp.

1. A feeling of being accepted and loved by those adults in their lives who exemplify to them the highest and best of life.

2. An ability to share affection.

3. Growing in and toward independence.

4. Happy experiences of companionship with their peer group.

5. Learning what will be expected of them as men and women (sex roles).

6. Development in the use and control of the muscles of the body.

7. Sense of achievement in becoming useful members of their society.

8. Accepting and carrying through responsibilities under their own power and direction.

9. Exploring, experimenting, and enjoying the world of things around them.

10. Growing in appreciation of those values which are highest in life and in their acceptance and practice.

The more a small group leader can know about each individual member of his group the better able he is to guide the experiences of the camper so he can achieve in those areas that are vital to him. Observing, talking with, working alongside of, sharing experiences within the group, all help the adult and child to know each other. One of the unique contributions of camp is provision for large blocks of time for just such living together.

Parents and church-school teachers oftentimes can help counselors know and understand children. Wherever possible a personal visit is best. Small group leaders may be able to visit with parents and teachers before coming to camp. Sometimes there is opportunity for a brief visit with parents when they bring their child to camp.

17

GUIDANCE MATERIAL

There is no single phase of life such as home, church, or school that can give a child the varied experiences he needs to grow into the sum total of what is known as wholesome Christian personality. It takes all these forces plus many others to accomplish such development. Camp is but one area of experience in the child's total environment. However, this does not minimize the contribution it can make but does more carefully define its special opportunities.

If the situations which require interaction of personalities are always the same, using the same or similar skills, the same or similar knowledge, then learning is in one direction. Consequently wise parents, teachers, and counselors seek for a great variety in the kinds of situations children are placed. The home provides certain kinds of opportunities, the church another, going to school opens a whole new world for children, and going to camp can be another totally different chance for growing and learning. New situations create new choices, new relations, new responsibilities. Children learn and grow when new choices are made and new responsibilities are accepted and achieved.

For any area of life, such as the home, the church, or the school to make its contribution to a person's life there must be much living and many experiences within its bounds. The same is true of camp. It is an impossibility for one single experience at camp to make every contribution to a camper's life that camp can make.

In order to provide a variety of experiences the Junior Camp Committee of the National Council of Churches of Christ in the United States of America has supervised the production of guidance materials for use by counselors in Junior Camps. These materials emphasize three areas of experience especially suitable to camp. They are (1) knowledge and appreciation of the world God has and is creating, (2) good stewardship relative to this world, and (3) living together in Christian fellowship.

Guidance material for the area "knowledge and appreciation of the world God has and is creating," is found in the junior camp manual *God at Work in His World* by Mary Venable. Conservation and stewardship are the emphases of the manual *Juniors in God's World* by Louise Davis.

THIS MANUAL

Living With Others is the manual which gives guidance for the third area listed above. It suggests activities, ways of guiding discussion, and worship possibilities. The resulting experiences should set up situations in which junior boys and girls may be led to realize through actual experience the validity of the teachings of Jesus in regard to the spiritual values in human relationships.

The suggestions given in this manual are in the form of resource ma-

18

terials. It is not intended that they shall be used in any particular sequence. However, the guidance materials for discussions and worship may be used in the sequence given in the manual if small group leaders so desire. It is conceivable that a group would spend several days exploring one discussion area with their worship experiences growing out of their discoveries and realizations. A careful study of the activities, possible discussions and worship suggestions will enable a counselor to draw upon the resources of the manual when there is readiness on the part of the group for a particular experience. This is an essential part of the pre-camp training.

The small group leader may wish to develop his own program, planning each day's activities with the children. The suggestions in this book then become resource materials for helping the small group carry out its own purposes and plans. A notebook may be used by the small group leader to record plans of the group and to help evaluate each day's experience. (See pages 115 to 120, this manual.)

THE CAMPER'S BOOK

There is a camper's book which accompanies this manual. Each camper should have a copy of this book. It is also titled *Living With Others*.

The camper's book provides guidance for devotional times and helps on camp skills. The resources in it may be used by the total group in times of work and devotion as well as by the individual camper.

SCHEDULE

One of the strong advantages of camp is long periods of time for living together in the small group. There are times, such as the opening council or the get-together for the day camp or mealtime in a resident camp, when the total camp group will be together. However the major portion of the time should be spent in the smaller groups.

Possible schedules are:

DAY CAMP

8:30 A.M.	Arrive at camp site. Many junior camp leaders prefer that boys and girls go straight to their own groups upon arrival at camp. However, in some situations where all do not arrive at the same time it may be wise to have a total group meeting at the beginning of the day.
8:30 A.M.— 9:00 A.M.	Experience has shown that fifty to sixty boys and girls in the total group make the best working situation. If it seems desirable this

group may meet at the beginning of the day. Such a time together gives opportunity for setting the tone of good fellowship for the day. It may be a good time for a brief moment of worship, a time of singing, or sharing between groups. This period together also provides an opportunity for discussing resources available, interesting things already discovered by the various small groups and sharing of information. Many small group leaders use this time to check their groups and to know who is present. A similar check should be made at the end of the day.

9:00 A.M.— 3:00 P.M.   Living in the small group. Each small group in its own camp site and busy about its own interests and activities. These may include explorations, cooking a meal, nature crafts, working on the camp site, and other activities. Lunch-time and rest period will be a part of this experience.

3:30 P.M.— 4:00 P.M.   The total group may or may not meet at the close of the day. This can be a time for checking in equipment, playing games, hearing stories, singing, or sharing experiences. It provides small group leaders an opportunity for checking on all campers. These things may be done in the small groups if counselors prefer and the children dismissed from there.

RESIDENT CAMP

7:45 A.M.   Rising Hour

8:15 A.M.   Breakfast

9:00 A.M.—12:00 NOON   Working in small groups. Part of this time may be used by the shelter group for cleaning up the sleeping area and caring for any responsibilities that the small group may have. Any total camp responsibilities such as sweeping the dining room or sterilizing the wash area may be cared for during this time. These duties may be cared for any time during the day. Some groups prefer to do them during the morning hours. Both in this morning block of time and in the afternoon block of time the small group may work on their campsite, do explorations, nature crafts, cook a meal, and other such activities.

12:30 P.M.	Lunch
1:15 P.M.— 5:30 P.M.	In the small group. Sometime early in the afternoon period there should be a time of rest. This may be on their blankets in the camp site or somewhere along the trail or on their beds in the shelters. Sufficient time should be included in the rest hour to bring the total number of hours for rest and sleep to twelve and a half hours.
6:00 P.M.	Dinner
7:00 P.M.— 7:45 P.M.	In the small group. Camp fires, storytelling, singing times, group discussion and worship are some of the opportunities of the evening period.
7:45 P.M.— 8:15 P.M.	In the Cabin
8:30 P.M.	Lights Out

THE SMALL GROUP

The small group is the eight to twelve campers and their leaders who live and work and play and worship together. There may be as many as four or five small groups in the total camp. Eight to twelve campers and two counselors make a small group. A more wholesome relationship is possible if half of the campers are girls and the other half boys. A woman counselor and a man counselor working together can more thoroughly meet the needs of the group.

There can and should be much freedom within the small group for planning its own activities and schedule. Ray and Betty with their group

worked out a schedule stating a preference of time for boating and swimming. Representatives from their group were sent with those from the other groups to work out a total camp schedule. Planning helps campers to be aware of their own needs as well as those of other groups in camp. They learn to work out their problems in

21

relation to and in consideration of members of their own group and of other campers.

Ray and Betty, mature counselors, could be depended upon to guide the group in making a plan for the day. Their schedule provided time for the physical needs of the group as well as for spiritual and emotional needs.

Freedom might well be the word written across the total camp experience. With mature small group leaders suggesting, guiding, counseling, sharing, there should be freedom to choose, freedom to plan, freedom to solve problems, freedom to accept and carry through responsibility, freedom to explore and to discover: freedom to learn.

3

David goes exploring

David quickly changed from his swim suit to camp clothes. Ray, Tom, and Cavin were waiting for him out on the rocks by the lake.

"Be sure to bring your knife," Ray called when he saw David start toward the rocks. "You will need it."

David checked his pocket. The new knife was still there, all sharpened, and ready to be used. David trotted out to the rocks and sat down beside Tom. This was a special committee from the discovery group. They were to mark a trail for an exploration trip the next day.

"Where will we go?" was Tom's first question.

"Will it be a long hike?" Cavin wanted to know.

"Can we see the ant hills?" David chimed in with his query.

Ray laughed. "Three questions all at once," he said. "Let's talk about them one at a time. How much time do you think we will have for the trip? Everything must be ready for the sleep-out before we go."

"The fireplace is finished," Cavin said.

"The tables are both up and ready," Tom added.

"The tarp isn't up yet," David remembered. "We will need it in case of rain."

"It will take us about half a day to put it up," Ray said, "so that leaves us about half a day for the trip. That tells us something about where we will go and how long a walk we shall plan. The ant hills are not too far away so, David, I think we can include them. Do you fellows know any other interesting places we can explore?"

The boys sat thinking. "How about the big quartz rock on the hill?" Tom asked.

"There's a water lily in bloom near the back end of the lake," Cavin added.

David could not remember anything. "Why can't we go looking?" he asked.

"That's a good idea," Ray said. "We can begin with the quartz rock and the water lily and mark our trail from there. We can include anything else we find. Let's go! Every fellow keep his eyes open!"

The boys followed Ray across the meadow. They began marking the trail at the bottom of the hill from their camp site. "This will be a good starting place," Cavin said.

Ray gave David the ball of twine to carry. Each time a trail marker was needed David cut a piece of twine with his knife. "It is important to have a good knife and to have it sharp," Ray said. "It is still more important to know when and how to use it."

David felt proud to have a good sharp knife. He was glad he was learning many ways of using it carefully and rightly.

The trail wound through the woods to the big quartz rock. After they had marked a stopping place they moved on alongside a stone fence. The boys found assorted kinds of lichens growing on the stones in the fence. "We can tell them about these," Cavin said. "They won't need to make a stop here."

Tom was the first to see the new hole in the hemlock tree. Ray looked carefully. "It looks as if a pileated woodpecker has been at work here," he said. "We will mark it for a stop. When we get back to camp we will stop by the library and check to be sure about the kind of woodpecker."

The boys marked a trail down near the back end of the lake so everyone could see the water lily in bloom. "If they will move quietly we might see a big frog sunning himself," Cavin said.

David's eyes opened wide at the sight of an ant hill. He had never seen so many ants in all his life. The hill was about a foot high and it looked as if millions of ants were running up and down its sides and in and out of the many openings. He got so interested he forgot to keep moving until he felt something crawling up his leg. "Ants," he yelled, "they're crawling on me!"

"Flip them off," Ray called to him laughing at the jig David was dancing, "and keep moving."

The last part of the trail took longer to mark because the boys did it with their compasses. It was the first time they had used compasses and it was slow work. It was a tired but happy committee that ended up back on the rocks near the lake.

"I didn't know there were so many interesting things around here," Tom said wonderingly. "Why, we have marked about umpteen stopping places!"

"This world is filled with interesting and marvelous things," Ray said quietly. "There are men who have given most of their lives to learning

24

about some special thing such as rocks, trees, shrubs or insects. After they spend years studying they still have much to learn."

"We learned in school about a man that just studied peanuts," Cavin said. "His name was George Washington Carver."

"He studied the sweet potato, too," said Ray. "Dr. Carver learned much about these two plants but never felt that he knew all there was to know. God has planned and created a wise and wonderful world for us. It provides us with food and shelter and clothing. There is also much that is beautiful for us to enjoy."

The boys sat thinking about what they had seen and about Ray's words.

"People become aware of God's greatness when they observe the wonders he has created," Ray went on. "Long ago a Hebrew psalmist said, 'O Lord, how manifold are thy works! In wisdom hast thou made them all; the earth is full of thy creatures.'" (Psalms 104:24.)

Only the sound of the waves against the shore and wind in the trees could be heard. The boys were so busy thinking about God's wise and wonderful plan they hardly knew when Ray began to pray, "Thank you, God, for a beautiful and interesting world in which to live. We thank you for a world in which we can work with you to grow food, clothing and to provide ourselves with shelter. Amen."

David looked at the blue sky overhead. He wondered how much there was to know about the sky and the clouds, and the sun. He smiled at Ray. He felt happy inside, happy about this great, wonderful world God had planned and created. He was happy, too, because he had used his new knife all afternoon!

DAVID LEARNS THROUGH
ACTIVITIES AT CAMP

After Jesus had chosen the twelve who were to work with him, there began a period of training for them. This training was given as that little group walked along highways, slept in the open, cooked and ate their meals, talked over their problems, raised questions, and worshiped together. Responsibilities were delegated, and each one grew in understanding of his place in the group and in ability to make his contribution. The rich fellowship these men had known in this small group with Jesus remained to strengthen them and to give them courage the remainder of their lives. Even Judas was not beyond its influence, for when the realization of the great wrong he had done came over him, he could not continue to live with his thoughts and memories. These men became great

25

because of the fellowship and training and inspiration they had in a small group with Jesus as leader.

Each small group leader in his humble way can work to the end of providing the boys and girls of his group with similar experiences of joyous fellowship. He can help them accept and carry through responsibilities for the good of the group. They can be helped to appreciate, understand, and accept Jesus' teachings about living with our fellow men. Moments of worship which arise out of such experiences can bring campers into the presence of God.

Camp has a particular contribution to make to growing boys and girls. If it is to make its contribution fully and well then those experiences which peculiarly belong to camp must be used.

A trip into the outdoors is a typical camp experience. The small committee that worked with Ray to mark a trail was carrying on some typical camp activities. Their learnings were multiple. First, they were carrying out a responsibility for the small group. David achieved personal satisfaction in using his knife. They all gained a new appreciation of the world in which they live. Last, but far from least, they were helped to express their thanks to God for creating such a wise and wonderful world.

What are some of the experiences that are peculiar to camp? Listed below are activities that can be used as means to the end of helping the Davids, the Toms, the Mirians, and the Carols who come to junior camp to grow in happy group ways. These activities are the living situations that create the necessity for individuals and groups to work out their problems of human relationships. These activities provide opportunities for growing in appreciations, understanding, and knowledge of this world in which we live. Small group leaders can set the tone and help to make the atmosphere, and consequently the growth of the campers Christian.

NAME TAGS

Whether members of the group know one another or are strangers, making a name tag seems always to have a popular appeal. It is a quick and easy way to get into a camp activity and provides some interesting experiences.

A small piece of wood may be sanded to a glossy smoothness. Cedar wood is a favorite with many because of its color and pleasant odor. However, any kind of wood may be used. Small pieces may be sawed and ready for the children to choose from upon arrival at camp or they may cut their own. The name may be written on with ink, carved with a knife, or burned with the sun through a magnifying glass.

The bark may be peeled from one side of a small branch and the name written with ink if the other kind of name tag is not possible. A strip

26

of birch bark glued to a heavy piece of cardboard makes an interesting tag.

A cord to swing the tag around the neck of the owner may be woven by the camper. Dried grasses, basswood bark or honeysuckle vines may be used in weaving or twisting such a cord.

There can be much wholesome sharing and good fellowship as a group works on name tags. It is a very fine way of getting better acquainted.

A CAMP SITE

One of the first activities for the small group will be to build a camp site where they can center each day's experiences. The campers will enjoy discovering possible places for such a site and discussing the advantages and disadvantages of each one. (See camper's book, page 9.)

There are no particular specifications for a camp site. It is helpful if there is water nearby that can be used for washing hands, dishes and for other activities. Firewood is another essential that is good to have close by. If there is to be a great deal of living in the camp area its accessibility is an important factor. How far will food for cooking out and blankets for resting have to be carried? This is an important item for juniors.

It is not good conservation to use one site until the ground is trampled hard and the surrounding plant life destroyed. Neither is it wise to allow the woods to become pockmarked by many campsites. Where many small camping groups use the site throughout the summer, the local management should work out a scheme of rotation of sites so some are closed out and new ones opened up. Each site should be allowed to return to its native state.

The space may need to be cleared of dead branches, underbrush, or rocks. A hand sickle can be used for cutting weeds and tall grasses. This clearing out activity may provide an opportunity for studying plant life. A wild flower guide may be on hand for checking on any flowers that might be near. One group that was camping in the early spring built their site around a jack-in-the-pulpit. Jack was still preaching when the campers left a week later! That is good camping conservation and appreciation of beauty!

Careful investigation must be made for poison ivy, and every camper should learn to identify it on sight. If the place is a wooded spot, some attention should be given to the trees. The root system may be in evidence, and this will be a good time to discuss proper care of the roots so they will not be harmed or hindered in their work for the tree. Closely related to this are the branches of the tree. Upon examination the campers can see that the lower branches of a tree get less sunshine and are consequently of less value to the tree. Therefore, if it is necessary to cut any branches from a tree, it should be these lower limbs. The shape of the tree is then unharmed, and only those limbs of least value are removed.

27

A fireplace can provide many happy experiences of cooking out for a group. Before building one talk with the campers about the necessity for having a fireplace that is safe and located in the open so the fire will not harm the surrounding plants and trees. Note any dry grass and leaves that should be removed to prevent the fire from spreading. (See camper's book, page 14.)

When the campers have chosen the spot for the fireplace, the space should be thoroughly cleared and a foundation of sand, gravel, or flat stones laid. A circle of rocks where rocks are available should be placed around the area where the fire is to be built. The outside of this circle of rocks may be packed with mud or sand or dirt, free from any material that would burn. A crossbar or tripod may be set up for holding pots when cooking. Provision may be made for putting out the fire after it has been used and for handling it should it start to spread. A bucket or can of water to sprinkle over the fire when it is no longer needed and a shovel for covering a spreading fire with dirt are examples of such provision.

Tinder, kindling and firewood may be gathered and stacked ready for use when needed. Tinder is inflammable material such as dry evergreen cones, dry weed stalks, sagebrush, and fat pine. Kindling that will burn long enough to ignite the firewood can be gathered and stacked with the firewood. Fat pine, paper birch, dead twigs, and small branches are best. Other soft woods cut into small pieces make good kindling. Wood for burning may be cut from dead branches and fallen trees. Sometimes special provision must be made for firewood. The wood pile should be covered to keep it dry in case of rain. This covering may be a piece of tarpaulin or canvas. (See camper's book, page 16.)

Tables may be lashed according to the needs of the group. Directions for lashing are given in the camper's book. (See camper's book, page 10.) The small group in which Ray and Betty were working made two tables, one near the fire to hold uncooked food and cooking utensils, another farther away for eating. This second one also served other purposes. It was a display place for specimens gathered on hikes and field trips. It

28

held the library books and other items brought out for each day's use. Flat stones may serve as seats, or a log may be rolled into a suitable position.

Hand-washing facilities may be rigged up somewhere nearby. A large size tin can may be tied to a nearby tree trunk or suspended from a lower limb. A small hole near the bottom of the can will let out a stream of water for washing hands. A nearby bucket, can or jug can furnish water for the hand-washing procedure. A small shelf may also be lashed to the tree or to a limb for holding soap and paper towels.

There are parts of the country where it is desirable to have some kind of shelter. Should the group plan to sleep out it will be wise to have shelter. This can be a tarpaulin or a lean-to. There are pictures in the camper's book showing various types of shelter.

MEALS OUTDOORS

There are several types of outdoor meals. It may be a bag lunch, a picnic, or a cook-out. Each type of meal has its place and is fun. Some or all of these experiences should be available to the campers.

The noon or evening meals are better for juniors to cook out. Active ten- and eleven-year-olds have hearty appetites. Especially is this true early in the morning after a long period without food. They are so hungry at breakfast they can hardly wait for food to cook. If breakfast is to be cooked out fruit and cereal can help to satisfy eager appetites so that the children can then enjoy cooking bacon and eggs and making good toast.

To plan and execute an outdoor meal democratically requires time. Individual growth takes place as youngsters have a part in the planning and as each one assumes his share of the responsibilities involved. Thus there is an opportunity for developing respect for the opinions and ideas of others and a chance to experience the real joy and satisfaction of co-operative group thinking and planning.

MENU. The first item to be discussed and decided upon is the menu. A discussion of foods, the way they serve the body and the variety needed in a balanced diet will help campers understand the importance of learning to eat and enjoy all kinds of foods. They may choose the menu for their meal outdoors in the light of this discussion. This needs to be done well in advance of the day for the cook-out. Advance planning allows time for checking equipment, amounts needed, and arranging for the food.

Meals cooked outdoors should be nutritious, well-cooked, and attractive. There is a variety of food that can be cooked and served out of doors. Too often, because of limited experience, both small group leaders and campers think only of roasting wieners or frying hamburgers when cooking in the open. Camp offers a wonderful opportunity for new experiences in cooking and eating. Cookbooks with simple but delicious recipes for outdoor cookery are available in many bookstores and from industrial organizations that produce foodstuffs and cooking accessories.

A few simple recipes are given below:

IRISH STEW (*serves 12*)

2½ pounds stew beef	12 carrots
12 onions	12 potatoes

Salt and pepper

Brown the meat in a frying pan in a little melted fat. Place browned meat in pot to be hung over the fire. Cover with cold water and cook slowly until tender about 1½ hours. Add vegetables and cook until tender. Season to taste and serve.

GROUND MEAT WITH VEGETABLES (*serves 12*)

2½ pounds ground steak or hamburger
Sliced onions, potatoes, carrots (approximately 12 each)
Butter
Salt and pepper

Arrange slices of potato, onion, and carrot on a large square of aluminum foil. Place a pattie of ground meat on the top. Cover with more vegetables. Salt and pepper to taste. Dot with butter. Wrap securely in foil and cook over hot coals. Turn frequently to prevent burning.

CAMPER'S SPAGHETTI (*serves 12*)

1½ pounds spaghetti	1 No. 2½ can tomatoes
9 slices bacon	3 or 4 large onions, sliced
3 teaspoons salt	3 cups diced cooked meat
½ teaspoon pepper	(canned will do)

1½ cups grated American cheese

Put spaghetti in a kettle of boiling salted water. Cook until tender, stirring occasionally. When tender drain off the water. Cut up the bacon and fry with the diced meat and onions. Add salt, pepper, and tomatoes and let simmer 10 to 15 minutes. Use as sauce over the spaghetti with grated cheese.

RING TUM DIDDY (*serves 5*)[1]

6 slices bacon, diced	1 No. 2 can tomatoes
2 onions sliced	1 No. 2 can corn
¼ pound cheese, diced	Salt and pepper

Fry the bacon and onions until brown, and pour off part of the fat. Add them to the tomatoes and corn and bring to a boil. Add the cheese and cook slowly until it is melted. Season to taste.

CAMPFIRE STEW (*serves 8*)[2]

1½-2 pounds hamburger steak	Salt and pepper
3 teaspoons fat	Kettle or frying pan
1 large onion, peeled and diced	Jackknife
2 cans concentrated vegetable soup	Spoon

Make little balls of hamburger adding seasoning. Fry with onions in frying pan, or in bottom of kettle, until onion is light brown and balls are well browned all over. Pour off excess fat. Add vegetable soup and enough water or soup stock to prevent sticking. Cover and cook slowly until meat balls are cooked all through. (The longer, the better.)

SOME MORES (*makes 12 servings*)

24 graham crackers
12 marshmallows
24 pieces milk chocolate candy

Place two pieces milk chocolate on graham cracker. Toast marshmallow; place on top of chocolate. Cover with second cracker.

MOCK ANGEL CAKE (*about 12 servings*)

2-inch squares of unsliced bread devoid of crust (day-old bread best)
1 can sweetened condensed milk
1 box shredded coconut

Place bread on sharpened stick and dip first in milk, then in coconut. Toast over fire. Milk and coconut are more accessible if placed in low bowls.

ORGANIZATION

After the menu has been chosen and the amounts of food have been estimated committees must be set up. The group may discuss the various jobs that will need to be done and set up committees accordingly. As each job is mentioned there should be a thorough discussion of the various responsibilities involved in carrying it out. Each member of the group must share in the work if it is to be a co-operatively executed cook-out.

Committees for a cook-out will vary according to the camp situation. Some possible committees with their duties are suggested below.

---

[1] From *Camp Counseling* by A. Viola Mitchell and Ida B. Crawford. Used by permission of W. B. Saunders Co.
[2] From *Your Own Book of Campcraft* by Catherine T. Hammett. Used by permission of Pocket Books, Inc.

Food Committee. Make a list of the foods and amounts of each needed. Plan for getting them assembled. In a resident camp this will mean a conference with the dietitian or director of the camp. In a day camp it may mean a trip to the grocery store to do the entire buying. Sometimes in a day camp the various items are portioned out among the campers to be brought on the day of the cook-out. Main items may be bought by a committee and smaller items portioned out.

This committee will pack the food carefully in bundles to be carried to the camp site by the members of the group. The necessary food items will be peeled, washed, and cut up before being packed. Upon arrival at the camp site the committee will unpack the food. They are also responsible for repacking any leftover food after the meal.

Cooking equipment other than that at the camp site is sometimes needed for cook-outs. The food committee will anticipate any such needs and will inform the equipment committee.

Equipment Committee. Make a list of all equipment needed. In a resident camp this committee will plan with the director of the camp a convenient time for checking out such items as are needed.

Equipment needs may include:

Can openers	Cooking utensils
Frying pans	Paper napkins
Water cans	Tin plates necessary for serving

Kettles for boiling (these may be large tin cans with wire handles)

Campers may or may not have their own tin plates, forks and spoons, and metal cup. Many camps ask that these be brought as a part of the camper's equipment. Other camps provide these items. The equipment committee can plan accordingly for supplying these needs.

The equipment committee will pack all equipment in bundles to be carried by members of the group. If the equipment calls for items found

32

out of doors, such as green sticks for roasting marshmallows, plan a time for doing this. Sometimes there is time to gather these while the food is cooking. There is also the possibility of involving the entire group in helping to gather such equipment items.

After the cook-out this committee will see that all equipment is cleaned and packed. They will return each item to its proper place or rightful owner.

FIRE COMMITTEE. This committee will need to decide how many and what kind of fires will be needed to cook the menu that has been planned. They will then be responsible for preparing safe areas for each of the needed fires. They will prepare the tinder, kindling, and fuel for the fires. (See camper's book, page 15.)

At the time of the cook-out this committee will carry the matches, build the fires and keep them burning as long as they are needed. They will see that all rules for fire safety are observed.

Buddy burners, tin can stoves, tin can boilers, and tripods are the responsibility of this committee when they are needed. The entire group may help in the making of these items under the direction of the committee. (See camper's book, pages 16-17.)

When the fires are no longer needed this committee will see that the fire is out. If buddy burners, tin can stoves, or tin can boilers are used, the fire committee will return them to their proper places clean and ready for use the next time.

COOKING COMMITTEE. This committee will help unpack the food at the camp site and place it on the table. They will cook those foods which need to be cooked and will lend individual aid and instruction wherever needed as the campers cook part of their own meal. They will serve the food and drink at the time of the meal.

Serving utensils will be placed wherever needed by the members of the committee. Sometimes individual foods must be divided into portions, such as breaking chocolate bars for "Some Mores" and the raw vegetables into servings. Wild flowers, pretty grasses, leaves, or an interesting stone may be used to make an attractive table.

When the meal is over the cooking committee will help pack the unused food and equipment. They will help to restore order to the camp site.

CLEANUP COMMITTEE. This committee will need to consider the menu and to anticipate the cooking and eating processes so they will be prepared for disposing of the garbage and other refuse. Containers for disposing of such items as peelings, paper napkins, tin cans, and other refuse may be conveniently located at the camp site. A member of this committee may be chosen to give the group careful instructions about putting all rubbish in the proper place.

After the meal is over this committee will be responsible for washing and sterilizing the dishes, burning the paper and other inflammable refuse. They will dispose of the garbage properly by either burying it or carrying it back to the kitchen or home for disposal. Garbage is never "just thrown away" but should be disposed of according to the policy established by the camp.

It may be necessary for this committee to work with the fire committee in cleaning buddy burners, hobo stoves, green sticks if they have been used, and storing them for future use. They may also assist the equipment committee in cleaning and returning cooking utensils.

An important item in the growth and development of sound personality is a sense of achievement. When a committee wins the approval of a group by carrying through their responsibility to a successful conclusion, there is a definite sense of achievement.

EVALUATION. A very important part of every camp cook-out is the evaluation of the entire experience. When the campers have finished their meal and the committees have completed their work, the group may sit around the fire or under a tree or in the camp area and talk over the experience.

This will be a time of joyous remembrance. They can laugh over the funny incidents that may have happened, recall the delicious flavors, express appreciation for work well done and generally relive the experience.

Part of this remembering may be of the mistakes that were made. Causes of the mistakes can be noted and the discussion may be centered for awhile on how they could have been avoided. It is careful evaluation of the causes and remedies that helps learning to take place. This need not be laborious but can be done lightly, easily and effectively.

34

Counselors need to guard against one person's being severely criticized by the remainder of the group. Great harm may be done to that person by such criticism, and it is not good for him or for the critics. It is quite a different matter if a camper himself says, "We could have had tomatoes in the stew if I had remembered to bring a can opener." Thus learning of a healthy and helpful kind takes place. The camper has evaluated his own behavior and has become aware that he could have better served his responsibility for the well-being of the entire group.

The cook-out experience may provide many opportunities for worship. Suggestions for such experiences are given in the section entitled "We May Worship Through a Cook-Out Experience," page 71.

SNACKS AND REFRESHMENTS. It is not always necessary to have an entire meal in order to have the fellowship of preparing and cooking something in the outdoors. Special snack treats such as ice cream made in a hand-freezer, blueberries gathered on a trip baked into muffins in a reflector oven, or popcorn popped over an open fire can provide a rich experience for the group.

Such snacks may be planned as a dessert for a sack lunch. They may be planned to be shared with another small group as a special treat or at the close of a time of fellowship together.

HIKES, EXPLORATIONS, TRIPS, RAMBLES

An integral part of the camp experience are trips into the outdoors for exploration, discovery, and enjoyment. These may be all-day trips when a sack or picnic lunch is carried, short trips for a single observation, or a ramble just for fun.

An example of an all-day hike is a small group that climbed a nearby mountain peak. They went up for a visit with the ranger who was in the look-out tower located on the peak during the fire hazardous time of the year. They carried lunches. After their visit they ate and rested before starting back to camp.

Another small group walked on tiptoe for about a hundred yards down a trail to see a red-eyed vireo sitting on her nest. The entire experience did not take more than half an hour but it was one of the most rewarding experiences of the camp.

It was a lazy summer afternoon. The small group had just put away their blankets following the rest time. "What is over that way?" one of the campers asked pointing off to the right in the direction of a pine thicket.

"Let's go see!" the leader responded and there followed a most delightful and unexpected ramble under the pines—brief, unplanned, worthwhile.

35

No matter what the length of the excursion into the outdoors nor when it comes in the total camp experience there must be a definite and worthwhile reason for undertaking it. It may be to see something interesting or beautiful in the world of nature, to visit an especially interesting spot to look for fossils, stones, unusual formations and the like, to visit with some person who can help answer their question, to open new avenues of interest or just for fun and relaxation. Sometimes the trip may be to help develop a skill such as the use of a compass. The group itself should determine when a trip is to be taken and the reason for going.

Certain safety precautions should be talked over and accepted by the group before a hike or trip is begun. Some of these are to stay within sight and hearing of the leader, to be aware of any dangers involved such as a high cliff, poison ivy, and similar risks. A first-aid kit should always be carried.

It is wise to evaluate each trip after it has been completed. Talking over experiences provides rich opportunities for learning to take place. Questions raised by some specimen, by some scene, or by some experience can often open the way for further exploration, study, or for worship.

Depending upon the local situation there are many things that can be observed and enjoyed on a trip. A few suggestions particularly pertinent to the theme and purpose of the manual are given here.

The campers may discover some of nature's varieties. They may look for variety in the colors of the birds, the flowers, and the soil. They may note the blue of the sky and the brown of the earth. They may examine the trees and note the various colors in the bark. The grasses have great variety in size and shape.

The protective coloring of the birds offers a beautiful study in variety. Some interesting examples are:

The blue of the male indigo bunting and the grayish brown of his mate.
The scarlet of the male tanager and the lovely olive green of his mate.
The white neck of the kingfisher that separates his head and body.
The white rump of the flicker that is concealed when he is at rest.

Wild flowers of the woodland and meadows provide an interesting study in size, shape, color, and foliage. As the campers discover these things, they will be interested to note that all these different flowers are growing in the same kind of soil and that each year they grow and bloom with the same color, size, and shape.

Rocks and rock formations make a fascinating study. There may be several kinds of rocks around the camp site. The campers may note the various sizes and shapes as well as the colorations. They may find some that have lichens and moss growing on them. If the camp is in a mountainous section, layers of rock may be observed.

Shells may be found along the seashore and sometimes in small streams. Hunting shells is a favorite pastime for all ages. Shells can open the way for a wonderful discussion of God's plan for small creatures. They can be made into an interesting display and can stimulate much research into kinds and ways of water creatures.

Another area of observation in the outdoors is that of the interrelatedness of various animals, plants, and other physical forces. Some of the more common examples of this interrelatedness are listed here:

1. All life depends upon the life-giving rays of the sun.

2. The bees gather nectar from the flowers and make it into honey which we enjoy. In gathering the nectar the bees carry pollen from flower to flower and fertilization, which means continued life to the flowers, takes place.

3. The trees take in the carbon dioxide from the air and return oxygen, which is needed by animals of all varieties for breathing. The cool, comfortable shade of the trees is appreciated in summer, and the warm homes built from their wood are enjoyed in the winter. Their nuts and fruits are fun to gather and delicious to eat.

4. The brooks and streams provide homes for water creatures, drink for thirsty animals, and moisture which adds beauty to the woodlands and meadows.

5. The grasses provide a beautiful green carpet for the earth, food for some animals, homes for many insects, and seeds for the birds to enjoy.

There is a negative aspect of nature's interrelatedness that may be observed and used in the discussions of this study. One of these may be a tree whose growth is stunted and inhibited because other trees are growing too close. In such a case the sun cannot shine through to its leaves and the larger root systems of the trees around draw most of the moisture and food from the soil. Such a tree is hindered in making its contribution to the world.

Some of the interesting discoveries of the trip may be brought back for a display of "Nature's Varieties." In making such a display care must always be exercised that rare flowers and ferns are not gathered. Leaves, bark, and other specimens should not be taken without careful attention that no harm is done to the mother plant. Through exercising such caution more conservation can be taught than could ever be done by word of mouth. The variety display may include such things as leaves, bark, grasses, rocks, flowers, feathers from birds, shells, ferns, mosses, and lichens.

The display when completed might be shared with another small group. Such a sharing would provide an opportunity for the campers to share with others their learnings. Even more important to the purposes of this study, it would provide an opportunity for friendliness and good fellowship between two or more small groups. Light refreshments such as lemonade and cookies or fruit might be served by the host group.

The Bibliography lists several books which give information about plants, rocks, insects, shells, and animals. These will be helpful on such hikes as described above. They may be brought to the camp site and kept in a sheltered place for reference.

NATURE MUSEUM

A nature museum is an excellent way for a small group to share with another group or with the entire camp group. The museum may be a trail about a mile in length, may be under the trees, or in a glen.

The museum may have a bulletin board with nature puzzles, riddles, creative writings, or quotations; directions to some interesting discovery; and a "What Is It?" shelf. Live pets that are properly housed may be kept here for a day or two for observation and enjoyment.

Equipment for predicting the weather may be a part of the museum. Directions for making such equipment may be found in the book *Adventuring in Nature* by Betty Price. (See Bibliography.) Chapter 7 deals with the weather bureau.

Articles fashioned from native clay, pine cones, and seed pods will be interesting items. Floral arrangements will add variety. Planters made from hollow logs or pieces of bark filled with plants from the woodland or meadow may give ideas for gifts to take home.

Notes pointing out some of the discoveries made by the campers may be placed along the trail for the enjoyment of others. Such notes as the following will add interest and enthusiasm when they are used to call attention to actual discoveries that have been made.

"Who were the world's first manufacturers of paper?" On the reverse side: "Wasps were the first manufacturers of paper. It is formed from chewed wood. There is a nest in the hemlock above your head."

"Yellow-billed sapsuckers are very fond of birch beer. The perforations on some of the birches along the trail were made for this purpose."

SWIMMING

The swim period is an important feature in many camps. With the water front personnel co-operating this can very profitably be made a small group activity. As such, the juniors will have wonderful opportunities for group planning and working out their plans in relation to the other groups in camp so as to have the different groups coming at different times.

With only one or two small groups in the water at a time there is the advantage of more individual attention for those who do not swim. There is also an opportunity for directed water games. The two small group leaders may lend assistance as they are able and are needed.

A SLEEP-OUT

Sleeping out is an exciting event for many junior campers because it is a new experience and has the sound of adventure. However, all juniors do not need to sleep out in order to experience high adventure in camp. Sleeping out can be a very wholesome and worthwhile experience if it is carefully planned and executed. A group cannot decide at three o'clock in the afternoon to sleep out that night and have a successful and happy experience. It takes mature and self-controlled small group leaders to guide a group of juniors through a successful sleep-out.

Many camps do not have available the essential equipment in sufficient quantities for a whole group to sleep out. This is a major consideration in making a decision about sleeping out. Another major concern is that of the small group leaders involved. Unless they have had adequate training and experience it will be difficult for them to make it a good experience.

The camp site must be ready to accommodate a group overnight. Some of the considerations are:

1. Is there sufficient shelter in case of rain?
2. Are latrines dug and ready for use?
3. Can a sufficient water supply for all needs be provided?
4. Is breakfast planned for and sufficient provision made for satisfying eager appetites early in the morning? Cereal and fruit help to take the edge off the hunger pains so juniors can happily and successfully cook the remainder of the meal.
5. Do the campers have ground cloths and bed rolls or sleeping bags as adequate protection against the moist ground and cooler temperatures of the nighttime? Slaters felt, available through contract builders, makes good and inexpensive ground cloths.
6. Are campers prepared to get the full amount of sleep or have a longer rest time the following day if they do not get the needed amount of sleep?
7. Is it an experience counselors will look forward to and enjoy?

39

Getting ready for a sleep-out can be an exciting adventure for a group. It provides excellent opportunities for working together for the good of all. Consideration for one another's well-being is the keynote of such preparation; thus, such an activity fits well into the purposes of this unit. The group may be divided into committees, each committee with definite responsibilities in preparation for the experience.

If a sleep-out is planned and carried out, the evening in camp provides an excellent time for a campfire or for a star study.

CHORAL READING

Choral reading is an excellent method of building a consciousness of the importance of a group working together. The real enjoyment comes from reading in harmony and rhythm with one another. It does not take many attempts for a group to learn that it is only as we listen to one another and read co-operatively together that we achieve pleasing results. Working together on a choral reading develops a new respect for the individual and his part in achieving success for the group.

Introduce the passage or poem that is to be used as a choral reading so there will be an appreciation of the background from which it came. Sometimes an experience of the group makes a good introduction. The selections from Psalms 65 and 104 as used in the discussion areas are examples of how this could happen. A story may introduce the selection, or it may grow out of a discussion.

After the passage has been introduced, the group may read it together. If it is from the Bible, they may use their own Bibles. Some of the references printed in the camper's book may be used. (See camper's book, pages 7 and 24.)

This first reading together will indicate to the counselor words that are difficult or whose meaning needs to be clarified. The passage may be reread several times to establish the natural rhythm. Then the youngsters may discuss it and decide how to divide the selection into parts for reading if it is not already divided.

Since there is very little difference in the tone quality of junior children's voices, the division into reading groups is simple. The group may be divided into two, three, or four sections according to the number of sections needed.

Solo voices may be chosen by the group as they listen to the various members read the solo parts. It is well to take turns with the solos until everyone who desires has had an opportunity to read them.

Reading chorally should be a pleasant experience. Drilling or working too long at a time dulls interest and natural enthusiasm. It is better to work awhile and then stop before interest wanes, then come back to the reading at another time.

CHANTING

Chanting is very closely related to choral reading. It is the step between speaking and singing. Early chants had many words sung on a tone that was very close to the speaking voice with a change in tone on the last three or four words. Sometimes this change meant going up a tone and down again or vice versa.

Sometimes a group can have a fine experience working out their own chant to a favorite psalm or one that has been given new meaning by some activity of the group. Old chants that have been used as aids to worship may be found in most hymnals. Three such chants are listed below along with the hymnals where they may be found. (See Bibliography.)

From *Hymns for Junior Worship:* "Our Prayer," No. 133; and "Glory Be to God on High" (verses 1 and 2), No. 123.

From *Singing Worship:* "O Come, Let Us Sing," No. 26.

NATURE CRAFTS

Working together on gifts to be shared with friends and family can be a pleasant way to spend a few hours or an afternoon in the camp site. The nature materials may be gathered on a hike or an exploration trip. Other necessary materials may be brought from the central source of supplies. There can be rich fellowship as a group works on these gifts. They may share ideas, materials and lend help whenever needed or desired. Some possibilities are listed below. Campers should be encouraged to think up their own ideas about things to make. These suggestions should be used only as starters for slow imaginations.

TWIG BRUSHES. Long, thin, green pliant twigs of willow, ash, hemlock or any other suitable twigs may be gathered on a hike or an exploration trip to make a brush. A stick of any desired length may be trimmed for the handle. A notch should be cut all around it near the base. Tightly bind the twigs to the handle directly over the notch. This should keep the brush from slipping off the handle. Trim the twigs at the top and at the bottom to make them neat and even.

BARK CRAFTS. The bark from several kinds of trees can be used in making useful as well as pretty articles. Birchbark is probably the best for such work but the American elm, hickory, several pines, poplar, cottonwood, white cedar, spruce, and hemlock may be used.

Great harm could be done to the forests if campers all across the country stripped bark for use in crafts. However, every year some trees are blown down by storms or cut in order to clear a site for building. The bark of such trees is seldom used. Such bark can be processed and kept

41

for years in a dry place. The bark may be stripped from the tree by making a straight cut down the trunk, then working the bark loose with a wedge. Spots where it is difficult to separate the bark from the wood may be gently pounded with a wooden hammer or maul.

After the bark has been removed soak it in hot water to make it pliable. If the bark is rough and coarse scrape the outer side to remove the thick roughness. Keep soaking it as it is being worked on to keep it pliable.

A sharp knife, a pair of large scissors, an awl for making holes in the bark and some large darning needles are needed for working with the bark. Lacing holes should be punched with an awl and inner bark or honeysuckle vine used for the lacings.

Bookmarkers can be made from bark. They may be made to fit the corner of a page or to lie flat in the place.

Book covers are also easy to make. Such covers should be a little larger than the books so they will slide on and off easily. Measure the size of the outside cover of the book including the back binding. Cut the bark approximately ¾ inch larger on all sides. Cut two pockets about 3 inches wide to fit each end. Punch holes around the edge. These may be about ½ inch apart and approximately the same distance from the edges. Put the end pockets in place and mark the holes to correspond with those in the cover. Lace the cover together with inner bark fibers or clean spruce or other evergreen roots. Soak these in water to make them pliable.

A small purse for change may be made from bark. These may be made much like an envelope and any desired size.

Charcoal Sketching. Small pieces of charcoal from the campfire provide an interesting sketching medium. If some really fine pieces of charcoal are desired pieces of thin, closely-grained hardwood may be placed in the fire. They should be covered with earth before they are consumed by the flames. Thus they become charred and ready for sketching.

A piece of sandstone makes a very fine sharpener. Any kind of paper may be used, drawing paper, wrapping paper or just plain newspaper.

Leaf and Flower Sketching. Leaves, flowers, and grasses of all kinds can be used in sketching. Soft pastel colors may be obtained from crushing these plants in the hand and using the plants as brushes on white drawing paper.

Stone Sketching. Some very interesting colors may result from rubbing various kinds of stones on paper. With a handful of small stones and a piece of paper a camper can often produce interesting designs. Use the stone as if it were a pencil or a piece of charcoal on white drawing paper.

PAPERWEIGHTS. Unusual or attractive stones may be gathered and cleaned. When thoroughly clean and dry, they may be varnished or shellacked to be used as paperweights.

WOODS PLANTERS. Hollow logs or heavy pieces of bark may be made into planters to be enjoyed while at camp or to be taken home. Much can be learned about transplanting plants from the woods or meadow into such planters and about the proper care of them afterwards.

Small planters may be made by lashing sticks together to form the size and shape container desired. These may be lined with moss before being filled with soil and growing plants.

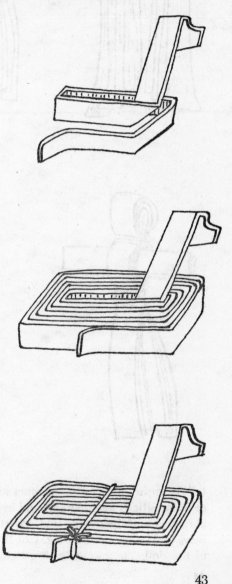

SOME "JUST FOR FUN" IDEAS. Cattail ducks were first made by the Indians for their boys and girls. Gather the full-grown cattails or rushes and let dry. Soak in water for a few minutes just before using. Fold one end of the cattail leaf to look like a duck's head. Leave some space between the head and the first fold for the neck. At the end of the neck, fold the cattail back and forth at right angles to the neck to make the body. The body may be four to six inches in length. The neck with the head at the top should be about midways of the body. Wrap the leaf around and around this fold until there is a broad enough base for the duck to float on the water. Tie it with a string of basswood fiber or a strong vine. Several of these ducks set afloat at one time give the appearance of a real flock.

Cattail or rush dolls were also made by the Indians for their children. These, too, can be done just for fun in camp. Prepare the cat-

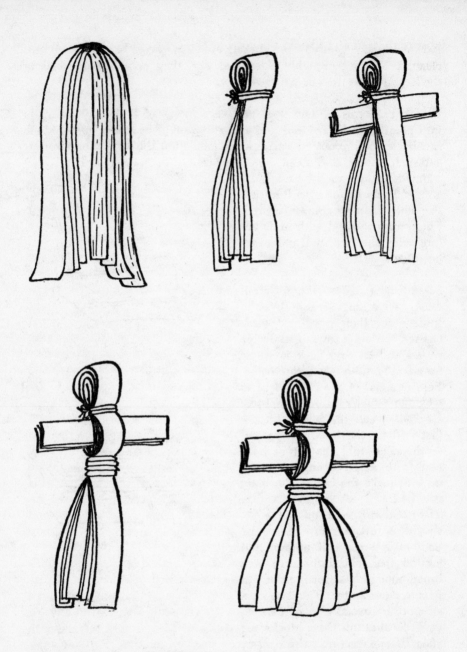

tails or rushes in the same manner as those for the ducks. Place a number of these cattails together and fold in half. Tie a string of plant fiber tightly about one inch below the fold. Insert another short bunch of cattails crossways just below the binding. Cut these to the proper length for the arms of the doll. Tie another string tightly just below the arms to make the waist of the doll and to hold the arms in place. Spread the lower part of the cattails to make the doll's skirt.

PINS. Acorns, hazelnuts and seedpods can be mounted in clay and made into pins. The fasteners for such pins may be secured from a craft supply house. They may be placed in the clay and allowed to harden there along with the design on the outer side. If the campers so desire these pins may be painted with a good grade of enamel.

CAMPFIRES

Camp would not be camp without a campfire and the fun and fellowship that accompanies such an experience. The campfire may be an experience of the discovery group or of the total camp group.

Wherever possible there should be times for both groups to have the fun, fellowship, and enrichment of a planned campfire experience.

A day camp group may have a campfire at the close of the day's experiences. This may be with the discovery group or can be a time of sharing for the entire camp group. Campfires are usually better later in the evening when it is cooler and darkness is beginning to come. A day camp group may come to the camp site later in the day on one or two occasions and stay for the evening meal and a campfire before going home. The campfire experience should be over in ample time for the campers to get home and to bed at their regular time.

A resident camp offers many opportunities for campfire experiences. The shelter group or the small group may have a campfire on the first or second evening in camp as a means of getting acquainted with each other. They may choose a place for the fire and begin early to learn safe fire building habits as well as the other learnings of the evening. This would be a good occasion for group singing, storytelling, planning together and learning about each other. Marshmallows may be roasted and enjoyed. A few moments of quiet worship might well come as the group sits around the dying embers of the campfire.

Either the small group or the entire camp might enjoy a "storyteller's convention" around a campfire. Both campers and counselors may participate in such a convention. If the total camp group is present, there will not be time for everyone to tell a story so some choices will have to be made ahead of time. Stories especially enjoyed around the campfire when the smaller groups are involved may be repeated for the larger group. The stories may be interspersed with group singing. The "convention" may be closed with a story of a worshipful nature told by a counselor or the director.

Sometimes a camp site itself has had an interesting history. Some camps or camping areas have Indian names or a pioneer background

45

that might be woven into a story. Most camps have some interesting stories about the selection, construction, and naming of the camp site. These can be shared around the campfire.

There can be no better atmosphere than around a campfire for talking things over as a group or for talking out problems and situations that have arisen through the day. Any of the discussion areas included in this manual could be discussed around a campfire by the small group. The warm glow of the fire seems to give everyone a feeling of acceptance and provides an excellent environment for thinking and talking together. Often such times of fellowshhip lead naturally to a moment of worship.

Small group leaders should be careful that any evening program close early enough for the campers to get to bed on time. The warmth and good fellowship of a campfire sometimes encourages a late bedtime. The time together will probably need to be only thirty-five to forty-five minutes if it is carefully planned.

STAR PARTY

An evening for studying the stars can be a thrilling occasion. The small group may take their blankets and go out where they can see the stars. One of the counselors or an invited guest may point out some of the major constellations. Some of the ancient stories about these constellations may be shared. There may be some campers in the group who can point out some of the constellations or share stories.

Stories and helps for finding the stars may be found in such books as:
The Sun and Its Family, The Earth's Nearest Neighbor, Beyond the Solar System, and *The Sky Above Us,* by Bertha Morres Parker.
Star Stories by Gertrude Chandler Warnte.

A fitting close to an evening spent with the stars would be a story of the Hebrew shepherds and their nighttime watches. "The Constant Star" or one of the other stories from the story section of this manual may be told. Psalms 8:1, 3, 4 may be shared during the course of the evening.

A study of the stars will of necessity have to come after dark. However, it should not cover too long a time. Thirty to forty minutes for the entire experience is ample. If such an evening is included provision should be made for the campers to get some extra sleep in the afternoon before they are to be up to see the stars. A later rising hour the next morning is another way of providing the essential sleep and rest. In either case, the amount of sleep should correspond to the estimated time the group will be up beyond the usual bedtime.

GAMES

Sometimes in the camp site, along the trail, or during a rest time in the midst of a hike there is the need and opportunity for a game. Playing together is good fellowship, and when done with fairness and as good sport, can help boys and girls to grow in Christian ways. A few games are listed here. Others may be found in books of games for boys and girls listed in the bibliography.

ROADSIDE CRIBBAGE [1]

Each person picks up ten small stones which he carries in his hand or pocket. As the group hikes along, the leader points out some nature object. Everyone tries to identify it in his mind. Then a volunteer is called upon to identify the object. When the correct name is determined, all those identifying it correctly in their minds may drop a stone. The one who has dropped all his stones first wins. All must agree to play fair.

SPOT SPY [1]

This game is great fun when a group is resting on a hike or loitering along the way. The leader says: "I can see five white oaks." The group is given one or two minutes to spot the white oaks. All those who see them may indicate this fact by sitting down, taking off their hats, or by some other agreed signal. All those who see the object receive a point.

GOOD TURN [1]

Set aside fifteen minutes on a hike, perhaps after lunch, for a "good turn." Each hiker is to do a good turn in the woods in that time and report on it or show it to the group. Clearing the trail of dangerous stones, burying trash or debris left by picnickers, removing a branch fallen on a plant, all constitute good turns. Watch the hikers lest in their zeal the good turn does more harm than good!

SOUNDS [1]

While resting on a hike, ask each person to write down every sound he hears during five minutes. The list will vary considerably, and it will be fun to see how many sounds are heard. You may hear the rustle of leaves in the wind, the chirping of a cricket, several bird songs, a snapping twig, the breathing of the group, and many other sounds.

HOLD THE FRONT [2]

4 to 15 players, ages 10 up. Players travel along a trail in single file. The leader asks a question about something observed along the trail, such as, "What kind of a tree is this?" "Point out three minerals in the granite." If "number one" in the line knows the proper answer, he holds

[1] From *Adventuring in Nature*, by Betty Price. Copyright 1939 by the National Recreation Association, Inc., and used by permission.
[2] From *Nature Lore Manual for Church Leaders*, by Reynold E. Carlson. Used by permission of the Division of the Local Church of the Board of Education of The Methodist Church.

47

his place in front. If he fails, he goes to the rear of the line. "Number two" then gets a chance to answer. Each player failing to answer goes to the rear of the line, and the person first answering correctly is "number one."

This is a good teaching game for a field trip.

CURIO COLLECTOR [3]

5 to 30 players, ages 10 to 15. The leader gives the group the name of something to be found, for example, a stump of a tree more than one hundred years old or a tree struck by lightning. The individuals scatter to find the object, the first finding it calling the rest of the group to see the curio. The leader then names the next object to be searched for.

FIND ME [3]

Any number of players, ages 10 up. A list of things to be seen in a given area is given to each player. He is to locate each of the objects without moving them and check it from his list. The game may last for the period of an afternoon or it may be used over a week's period in camp. At the end of the period the leader would go out with the group and find all the things on the list so that each person can determine the correctness of his list. The list might include such things as an oriole's nest, cattails, tent caterpillars, three kinds of oak trees, limestone ledge, brake fern, and so on.

SINGING

One of the joyous experiences of camp is group singing. Along the trail, in the camp site, around the campfire, grace before meals, the time of worship are all opportunities for singing. Gone is the time when a special person was provided on the camp staff to have charge of the music. Every counselor and camper can help with the music. It is a time of joyous fellowship and anyone can start or teach a song.

[3] From *Nature Lore Manual for Church Leaders*, by Reynold E. Carlson. Used by permission of the Division of the Local Church of the Board of Education of The Methodist Church.

The same care is given to the choice of songs as is given to any other materials used in the Christian nurture of growing persons. Such questions as the following will help in choosing songs for use in the worship experiences: Are the concepts in keeping with the teachings of Jesus? Are the words within the experience and understanding of the group? And does it help to express a feeling or emotion in keeping with the group's experience?

In choosing fellowship songs the same care will be used. Questions such as these will help guide counselors in the choice of fellowship songs:

Does it express right attitudes toward people?
Is it wholesome fun?
Is the music within the voice range of the group?
Is the music good?

4

A time for David to think

Ray and David were leading the way along the trail. All at once Ray stopped and held up his hand for silence. He turned his head to one side and stood listening. Everyone stopped and waited eagerly to see what was happening. When all was still the boys and girls heard a low humming sound.

"Wait here while I go looking," Ray said. The campers could hear him moving quietly around. It was not long until he motioned for the boys and girls to join him. They left the path and walked through the under-brush. When they came close, Ray pointed to a big old gum tree.

"A bee tree," he said, grinning from ear to ear.

"What's a bee tree?" came in chorus from the whole group. Their faces looked surprised and curious.

"I never heard of a bee tree," David said wonderingly.

"A bee tree is a hollow tree chosen by a whole community of bees for their home," Ray explained. "Watch and you will see some of them going in and out of that big split in the side."

Sure enough, as they watched they saw many bees going in and out of the hollow tree. "Is that what makes the humming sound?" Carol wanted to know.

"Partly," Ray nodded. "Let's sit down here in the shade and talk about it. We need a rest anyway."

Everyone sat down, each one trying to get as close to Ray as possible

and still keep the bee tree in view. When everyone was comfortable Ray began.

"Bees live in communities. Each community has many, many bees but only one queen bee. She lays all the eggs from which other bees are hatched. Many of the bees in a community are worker bees. Some of these build wax cells. Others use their long tongues to collect nectar and pollen from the flowers. This is made into honey. Still other workers are busy packing the honey and pollen into storage cells. This is food for the bees to eat in the wintertime. Some of the workers use their wings as fans to keep the home cool. Each community of bees must have a home."

Mirian's eyes were shining, "I know!" she began to clap her hands. "I know! A bee tree is the home of a community of bees."

"You are right," Ray smiled at her. "These are wild honeybees. They like a hollow tree for their home and that big old gum tree is just right."

David was thinking about all those worker bees. "There sure are a lot of worker bees," he said out loud. "What if one bunch of them decided to go on a strike?"

Everyone laughed at the thought of bees on a strike. "I guess that would be a pretty serious problem," Ray said, "but somehow or other those bees never go on a strike. Each group seems to know that their work is important and they get it done. Each group makes their contribution for the good of them all."

There was a thoughtful expression on David's face. "Just like our group working on the camp site," he said wonderingly.

Ray nodded his head. "Yes, we had several groups of workers when we were building our camp site. Each group was important and the work they did made it possible for all of us to have a camp site to enjoy."

Betty had been listening quietly all this time. "That is God's plan," she said softly. "Each person has some contribution he can make better than anyone else."

"Like Mirian's voice to carry the tune when we are singing," Ray said.

"Tom to show us how to row a boat," Cavin added.

"And Carol to cook bread twists," Tom grinned.

"The way David can use an ax," Betty smiled across at him as she said it.

"There is a verse in the New Testament about living together with others," Ray spoke thoughtfully and quietly. "This verse says, 'Do not neglect to do good and to share what you have.' (Hebrews 13:16.) I like to think this means for each person to share with others the things he can do best."

"Paul once wrote something about the way we do our work," Betty said, reading from another place in the New Testament. "Once he wrote,

51

'Whatever your task, work heartily.' (Colossians 3:23.) I'm glad every-one is important and that everyone has some contribution to make."

The group sat thinking. David looked around the circle. He remem-bered some of the ways each person in the group had been helpful. "Even the girls," he said so softly that only Betty heard. She smiled and laid her hand on his shoulder.

"Well, there is still trail to be covered before we are back in camp," Ray said, getting up from the stone on which he had been sitting. "Let's get moving."

David was the last to fall in line. He turned for one more look at the bee tree. He smiled as he saw the workers moving in and out. "Each one knowing what he can do and working heartily," he said softly as he started down the trail.

TALK IT OVER TIMES

There are many problems involved in living together happily as a group. Situations will arise along the trail, in the campsite, while play-ing a game or at almost any unexpected time when things need to be talked over. It is in such discussions that opportunities arise for gaining new understandings and insights into human relationships.

Ray and Betty used the opportunity afforded by the discovery of a bee tree to talk over an important part of God's plan for each individual. They helped their group to grow in appreciation of the contribution each individual can make to the welfare of the whole group. They also in-troduced the thought of each individual being responsible for seeing that he makes his contribution.

The purposes of this manual are aimed at learning important considera-tions about living together in happy ways. The activities suggested should provide many opportunities for the group to think about some of the problems that arise when persons live together. The resulting discussions should help the boys and girls grow in Christian attitudes and habits.

Worship may or may not result from these discussions. Ray's and Betty's group were very close to worship as new realizations came to them out of the discussion about bees and each one making his contribution. Sometimes the worship experience will come at a later time after the campers have had more time for thinking about it.

It would be an impossible task to try to imagine all the situations that might lead into specific discussions about Christian ways of living together. Some that are particularly pertinent to the theme of this manual are given below. Some guidance is given as to how they might be developed with a small group.

It is quite conceivable that a group could spend a great deal of time discussing one or more areas with which they are especially concerned. The counselor's purpose is to help boys and girls to grow in Christian ways. Guidance materials are only a means to that end and should be used as such.

Worship suggestions are included along with the possible discussions. This does not mean the discussion and worship should always come together, although they may do so frequently. These suggestions are intended to give guidance for both discussion and worship and to be used as needed.

Small group leaders using this material will want to read these possible discussions over carefully. Associate those that seem most pertinent to the situation in which they will be working with the possible experiences of the group. Rephrase or rethink the guidance material so it will be better suited to the local situation and group.

The two counselors who are working with a group may share the responsibility for these times of talking over problems in Christian living. Each can then study more carefully those for which he is responsible and will consequently be better prepared.

POSSIBLE DISCUSSION AND WORSHIP AREAS

I LIVE IN A GROUP

DISCUSSION AREAS

What is it that makes a family or group of people happy together?
How did Jesus guide people into happy ways of living and working?
What shall we do about teasing; borrowing; tempers?
Are health rules important in camp?

DISCUSSION

Each one of you came to camp from a home. Some of you came from big families and some from small families. Some of you may have only one or two persons in your family.

What do you think makes a family a happy family? Does the number of people in it have anything to do with whether it is happy or not? Sometimes a large family can be very happy, and sometimes the same size family can be very unhappy. What makes the difference?

While we are at camp this will be our home. The group with whom we work and play and live will be our camp family. We can make it any kind of family we want it to be. What kind of family do you want our camp family to be?

For many, many years people have been trying to find happy ways of living together. That has always been a very important problem. Jesus knew that when he was living in Palestine. He gave much help to those who want to live together in peace and happiness. We can find what he taught and practiced in the Bible.

Study Jesus' Teachings About Living Together. Read the following references from the Bible. Discuss the meaning. Does it have any guidance for happy camp life?

> Matthew 7:12
> Matthew 22:35-40
> Matthew 25:34-40
> John 15:12
> Luke 6:27-36

It will help to clarify the meaning if the boys and girls try to paraphrase these verses. They may do this individually, as a total group, or in small committees.

Discussion. Are these good rules for living together in the world of today? Why do you think so?

When boys and girls live together at camp they sometimes have problems. One of these problems is teasing. There are different kinds of teasing. Do you know what they are? How does teasing for fun make you feel? How does the teasing that hurts make you feel? How can we tell the difference in teasing for fun and teasing that hurts? Do you think there is any place in Jesus' rules for teasing? What shall we do about teasing in our group?

Sometimes when you are among campers you hear someone say, "Lend me your knife," or "Lend me your bar of soap." Is there a difference in "lending" and "giving"? What do you think about lending? Do Jesus' rules about living together give any help about this problem? How do we want to handle lending between ourselves?

With so many people living together in one group it will be easy for one person's belongings to get in another's way. There are some who get angry when that happens. Does that help? Is there a better way of settling the problem? What shall we do about it?

No matter where we are or what we are doing we need strong, healthy bodies. That is especially true at camp. There are certain health rules that help us keep well if we practice them every day. Can you name some of them?

Junior boys and girls need twelve to twelve-and-a-half hours' sleep each day. They need a rest period in the middle of a busy day. Is that an important rule for us to remember? What if you do not want to sleep that much or to take a rest period and your neighbor does? Is there anything in Jesus' rules that helps you to know the Christian thing to do? Which do you think is better, co-operating with each other and with the laws of health or each one doing as he pleases? Why do you think so?

The laws of health also say something about cleanliness. What do we need to remember about clean bodies? How about a clean camp site? Is it important to remember these rules every day? Why?

WORSHIP

The campers may study the words of the hymn "The World One Neighborhood" from the campers' book.

Jesus' rules for living together speak often of "loving" one another or showing "love." What do you think love means? How can we show someone that we love him?

Paul was one of the best followers Jesus ever had. He has helped many people to understand the meaning of love in one of his writings. Let us read Paul's description of love. (Read selections from 1 Corinthians 13.)

Prayer. The prayer may give thanks for the happy experiences the group has already had together. It may ask for God's help in keeping Jesus' rules for happy group living.

MY GROUP LIVES WITH OTHER GROUPS

DISCUSSION AREAS

What are some of the camp facilities that everyone will be using?

What problems may arise when several groups need to use the same swimming pool, craft materials, ball of twine, and so forth?

55

How can these problems be solved?

What are the Christian ways of solving them?

DISCUSSION

There are several groups that will be living together here in this camp area. There are some facilities that everyone will want and need to use. Can you name some of them?

What would it be like in the swimming pool if everyone went swimming at the same time? Could there be games? How about those who do not swim but would like to learn? Would it be easy for them to learn with everyone in at the same time? How about the lifeguard trying to keep everyone safe if the pool is full of people? What do you think would be a good way to handle the swim period? Is there a way of working it out so there will be only a few in swimming at one time?

Do you like to work in a craft room or with craft materials or tools that are out of order? Is it easy to find tools that are never kept in the same place? Is it necessary to have that kind of a situation? How can it be prevented? Which makes for happy group living?

There is a story in the Old Testament about many groups of people working together to solve a common problem. Listen to the story and find out how they worked out their problem.

Tell the Story. Jerusalem was the capital city of the Jews. They loved the city very much because, not only was it the home of their king, it was also the capital city of their religion. It was here that Solomon had built the beautiful Temple for the worship of God. Every Jew hoped to be able to come at least once in his lifetime to worship in the great Temple for one of the specially high and holy feast days.

Because kings and countries knew no better ways of showing their power than to go to war, there was often the sound of marching soldiers and cries of battle. To capture a nation's capital city and burn it to the ground was to be a successful warrior.

Much to the sorrow of the Jews their beloved city of Jerusalem was captured. The Temple was destroyed, the walls and gates around the city were knocked down, and many of the buildings burned. It was a day of sadness and disgrace for the Jews.

Slowly those who were left in the city repaired their homes or built new ones altogether. As the years went by some who had been driven out by the conquering king were allowed to come back. They, too, found homes for their families.

All the Jews were distressed that there was no longer a Temple where they could worship God. "We must rebuild the Temple," they said and went to work to get it done. Once again the great doors of the Temple swung open each day for worshipers to enter.

Only the walls and gates remained in ruins. They were charred reminders to the people that no longer was their city a respectable one nor a safe one in the eyes of the neighboring countries.

Nehemiah, a Jew, was serving in the court of the Persian king. He heard from friends who had been there that his beloved Jerusalem was still in disgrace. He determined to do something to help. First, he asked permission to return to Jerusalem for awhile. He was given this permission.

In Jerusalem, Nehemiah studied the city to discover all the things that needed to be done. Because he wanted to be sure about his plans before he shared them, he kept his movements a secret. He rode around the city wall by moonlight so no one would know what he had in mind. At the end of three days he was ready to talk with the people.

Nehemiah knew all that needed to be done and he had thought of a very good plan. When he stood before the people he made a very stirring speech. He told them that by working together as small groups they could repair the walls and gates. As the people listened they became excited and thrilled.

"Come, let us build the wall of Jerusalem that we may no longer suffer disgrace," he said to the people.

Their eyes were shining with new hope and enthusiasm as the people answered. "Let us rise up and build."

Nehemiah's plan was for each family to join with the other families nearby. These small groups would then work on the part of the wall that was nearest to them. It was a new and different plan. The people liked it and set to work with enthusiasm.

The rubbish was cleared away. Those stones which could be used again were saved. New ones were brought for those that had been destroyed. Day by day the wall became stronger and more secure.

Special groups took over the task of rebuilding the different sets of gates that opened into the city. Strong beams were brought to hold the heavy gates. As the walls were built up, the openings were closed with big gates.

Jerusalem was no longer charred and in ruins. Each small group of people had done its part in rebuilding the city walls and gates. Once again they looked and spoke with pride of their beloved capital city. Once again it was a city where the tribes could go for the worship of God. (Based on Nehemiah 1-4)

Discussion. These people learned something very important about working together. They discovered that when small groups work together everyone can benefit. It is a wise and good plan.

What would have been the result if one small group had refused to do its part? How would the other groups have felt toward them? How would they have felt about themselves?

Our camp is made up of small groups. There is some work that each small group will need to do in order to keep the camp clean, the tools and craft materials in order and everyone safe and happy. Each group can contribute to the good of the whole camp.

Worship

Nehemiah and his friends and neighbors discovered that just talking about a problem did not get it solved. Something needed to be done about it and they were the ones to do it. They also found that there was a job for everyone to do. If any one group shirked their duty then an important part of the work did not get done.

John was one of the early Christians. Once he wrote these words, "Let us not love in word or speech but in deed and in truth." (1 John 3:18.) It is not enough to say that we love our friends. We must show them in the things we do. We can show our love by taking care of our responsibilities for the work that must be done for the good of all. This may be in our family, in our small group, or in the total camp group.

Jesus is an example of one who always accepted his responsibility and did his share of the work. He loved "in deed and in truth."

John Oxenham once wrote a book of poetry describing the life of Jesus. Some of the lines of poetry in that book describe what Dr. Oxenham thought Jesus was like when he was about your age. As you listen to these lines try to imagine what it would be like if your group were made up of persons like this.

> He sported with the village boys and girls
> Among the vines and olives of the hills,
> Nor lacked in boyish mischiefs with the rest.
> He loved the games in street and market-place,
> And laughed and splashed and shouted in the stream.
>
> . . . .
>
> Nature he loved as kinsman loves his kin,
> And held all beasts and birds and flowers and trees
> In sweet esteem . . .
>
> . . . .
>
> His trade was humble, but he gave to it
> Such pride of high endeavour that his skill
> Won fame beyond his borders, and men came
> From far to buy his plows that never turned
> Poor furrows; and still more his perfect yokes.
>
> . . . .
>
> His face was winning in its gladsomeness;
> The children crowded round him as he toiled,
> Begging for stories; and when business pressed,

58

He set them working, to their delight,—
Clearing his shavings, sorting out his nails,
Helping the carpenter, and claiming toll
Of longer stories when his work was done.

. . . .

He taught a new sweet simple rule of Right
'Twixt man and God, and so 'twixt man and man,—
That men should first love God and serve Him well,
Then love and serve their neighbours as themselves.[1]

Prayer. The group may give thanks for the example of Jesus as one who accepted his responsibilities and did them cheerfully and happily. They may pray for help to learn their own responsibilities for the total group and to do them well and with pleasant attitudes.

I LIVE IN A COMMUNITY

DISCUSSION AREAS

How is camp like a community?

What should be my attitude toward the property that is owned and used by the total group?

What should be my attitude toward property that belongs to other campers?

Does the Bible give any help on these problems?

DISCUSSION

How many groups do we have in camp? What is there about several groups living together in camp that is like a community?

All the families in a community use some of the same facilities. The water they use in their homes comes from the same source. They walk and drive their cars over the same streets. They picnic in the same park. The children go to the same school. Many of them go to the same church. There is often only one hospital.

How does your family feel about your water supply? Why is that such an important item to them? What would be the reaction in your community if someone started digging up the streets? Does the fact that these utilities belong to everybody make any difference in the way we treat them?

We have some items that are "common property" here at camp. Can you name some of them? Are they important items for each group and each individual in camp? Why do you think so? How should we treat them?

There are not only items that are common property for those here in

---

[1] From *Gentlemen—The King!* by John Oxenham. The Pilgrim Press. Used by permission.

camp, there are also items that belong to those who live in the neighborhood. How do you think a farmer feels about his fences; his cultivated fields? What should be our attitude toward property that is important to others; do we have any responsibility for them? What should we do about campfires; why?

Every community has some arrangements for keeping itself clean and in good operation. If our camp is a community we should have some plan for keeping it clean and in good running order. What can we do to keep our camp running smoothly? One group of campers made this list. Do you think it is a good one?

> Use tools rightly and carefully.
> Take turns using tools when the supply is limited.
> Do not damage or misuse property.
> Be very careful not to contaminate the water supply.
> Watch all campfires so there is no danger of their
> spreading or causing a big fire.
> Always play safety first.

WORSHIP

There are many stories in the Bible about people who had problems in living with others. There is much help there for us. Let us find some of the references that give special help for living in a community. These we can share with each other. As we share them let us think what they could mean for us here in our group at camp.

> Mark 3:33b-35.
> Romans 10:12.
> 1 Corinthians 10:24
> Acts 10:34-35.

The hymn, "The World One Neighborhood" from the Camper's Book may be studied and related to the Bible material. It may be sung as a prayer hymn.

I LIVE IN A WORLD OF VARIETY

DISCUSSION AREAS

What are some of the varieties to be found in the world around us?

Do these varieties of plant life serve any useful purpose?

What other evidences are there around us of the great variety of living creatures?

Is there a reason for the many different kinds of animals?

DISCUSSION

There are many plants all around us. Take a good look at some of them.

60

Each plant has a root system and a stem. Are the roots all alike? Does each plant have the same size stem? Think about some of the plants such as beets, onions, potatoes, that store their food in their roots. What useful and good purpose do they serve?

Do you know some plants where the stem is important? How about sugar cane, rhubarb, asparagus? In still other plants it is the leaves or the seed pods that are important. Can you name some of them?

How dull and uninteresting would be our meals if we had only one kind of food to eat! If we had only roots or stems or leaves or seed pods we would have some variety but how much pleasanter it is to have them all!

Let us move from food plants to trees. How many different kinds of trees can you see in camp? Think about some you know. Which trees help to provide food? How many different kinds of fruits and nuts can you name? Trees help in many other ways. Do you know some of them? There is lumber for building, pulpwood for paper, and so on.

Trees provide beauty—some because of their shape, some because of their blossoms, some because of their leaves. How many can you name? Can you think of other services trees provide?

Would you enjoy looking for birds or listening to their songs if they were all alike? If there were only one kind of flower, we would soon tire of it.

Do you have an animal pet at home? What are some of the things you enjoy about your pet? There are many species of animals. Some are known as domestic animals and some as wild animals.

Domestic animals are useful to man in many ways. Some of them provide food, others help carry on man's work. Some are pets and provide good company and protection.

Wild animals are useful, too. Sometimes they provide food. Have you eaten meat from such animals? Do you know other ways in which wild animals are useful or helpful?

Everywhere we look in the world about us there is variety. This variety makes the world a more beautiful place in which to live. It provides people with interesting and different foods. The great variety of animals makes it possible to have help for getting work done and companionship for men. God's plan is wise and wonderful.

Worship

Long ago the Hebrew people lived much in the outdoors. They were aware of the great variety of plants, of trees, of weather, of birds and all the other living, growing things. They were pleased and happy with God's plan for such varieties all around them. They sang praises to God for them.

One of the psalms of praise to God for all these varieties in the world is Psalms 148. Read it to find some of the varieties mentioned.

Choral Reading. After the group has read the psalm and discussed its meaning they may read it chorally. Help for doing choral reading is given in the section on activities, page 40.

The group might enjoy writing a psalm of their own, praising God for some of the varieties they are enjoying in camp.

Prayer. The group may compose a litany of thanksgiving for the varieties of plant and animal life that are found in the world. The litany may be made by each member of the group naming some special item for which he is thankful and the entire group singing or speaking a response.

I LIVE IN A WORLD OF DIFFERENT PEOPLE

DISCUSSION AREAS

Are there ways in which I am like other people?
What are some of the ways in which I am different from others?
Is it good to be different from others?
What is God's plan for variety in persons?

DISCUSSION

There are ways in which all people are alike. Can you think of some of the ways in which you are like every other member of this group? Each one has a body in which he lives and moves and has his being. Each body is built according to the same pattern with arms, legs, a head, and so forth. Each body needs food and clothing and shelter. We like to play, to have fun and to have friends.

There are ways in which we are different from each other, too. Let us look carefully at each person in our group. Each member of our group has two eyes, but can you find two pair of eyes exactly alike? Count and see how many colors you can find in the eyes of this group. Look at the shape of the eyes. How many are shaped exactly alike? Are they all the same size?

Each one has hair on his head. Does everyone have the same color of hair? How many colors of hair can you count? Do some have curly hair? Is some hair straight?

Most of those in our group are about the same age. Are they all the same size? Do you think we would all weigh the same? Some are tall, some are short. Some are heavy, some are light.

If we could travel on a magic carpet around the world, we would find other boys and girls just like us, each one needing the same things we need, each one enjoying many of the same things we enjoy. We would find them different from us in some ways, too. Do you know some person from another part of the world? How is that person like you? How is that person different from you? Even people from nations in the same part of the world differ: Do you know some of them and how they are different?

A Helpful Book. Eva Knox Evans' book *All About Us* is a delightfully written book giving information about people. It tells in clever language of their basic similarities and differences. It provides excellent information for this discussion on people and how they are different. Portions of it may be read aloud in connection with this discussion. The first two sections are especially good at this point. If time is limited, use the second section "About the Way We Look" which starts on page 23.

WORSHIP

Help from the Bible. There were some problems in the time of Jesus because the people were different. The people who lived in Samaria were not liked by those who lived in Palestine. There is a story in the New Testament that tells how Jesus treated a woman from Samaria. Let us read that story to discover what Jesus did when he met a woman who was different.

Read John 4:5-15, 23-26. What was Jesus' attitude toward the woman who was different?

Peter was one of Jesus' disciples. He was troubled about how he should treat those who were different from him. God helped him to find an answer to his problem. The story of Peter's discovery is in Acts 10:1-5, 9-19, 21-28, 34-35. Peter speaks about his important discovery in verses 34-35. Read it carefully. What did he discover?

Once when Jesus was talking with his friends he gave them two commandments which he felt were the most important of all for us to keep. Let us read them as they are written in the Bible. Matthew 22:37-39. How does Jesus say we must feel toward our neighbors? Does he say anything about how they shall look or what size they should be? Do you think those things make any difference to him? Should they to us?

Prayer. There may be thanksgiving for the varieties of people God has created. There may be gratitude for the differences in the members of the group which make them more interesting and stimulating to one another. This prayer may also ask for God's help in learning to live happily with all kinds of people.

I THINK DIFFERENTLY FROM OTHERS

DISCUSSION AREAS

What are some of the ways in which people think and act differently from each other?

Why do people think and act differently?

What is the Christian way of handling differences of opinion?

When we look around here at camp we find great variety. There are many kinds and colors of birds. There are many sizes and shapes of trees. The flowers are different in size and shape and color. Everywhere we look we see differences in the world of nature. That is the way it should be. That is God's plan.

People are different, too. Some have blue eyes and others have brown. One has black hair and another has yellow. There are tall people and short people. Everyone we meet is different in some way. That, too, is God's plan for people.

When we listen to people talking we soon learn that they do not think alike either. Some believe one way and some another. One person likes one thing, and another does not like that thing at all.

Will each one of you name your favorite color? Do you have a reason for especially liking that color? Which color do you like least? Do you have some reason for disliking that color? Is there any particular reason why we should all like the same color; or dislike the same color?

If we were to talk about homes or churches or schools, each one in this group would have one special home or church or school that he liked best in all the world. Why would he think so? Would he be right? Is there any reason for being angry with one person because he likes his home better than mine? Should I try to make him like mine better than his; why?

It is not difficult to understand why people think differently about such things as colors and homes and churches and schools. Sometimes it is hard to understand why people think differently about a way of behaving or about another person. What should we do then? Does getting angry help? Does arguing help? What should I do when the opinions of others do not agree with mine? Talking it over often helps. Sometimes one or the other of the persons does not know some information that would help them to understand the situation. Often there is help in the Bible.

There have always been differences in people's thinking and feeling and acting. Paul once spoke of the way people feel about the days of the week and of the year. He wrote: "One man esteems one day as better than another, while another man esteems all days alike. Let everyone be fully convinced in his own mind. He who observes the day, observes it in honor of the Lord." (Romans 14:5, 6.) Paul did not feel that it made any difference how we felt about the day. The important thing was to live each day so God would be honored with our behavior.

People have always thought and behaved and looked different. It has been hard for them to know how to work with one another because of these differences. Jesus knew this, and in talking with his friends he had something to say about how we should feel toward others and how we should treat them. Do you remember the two great commandments Jesus gave? One of them is concerned with our feelings toward others. Matthew 22:39.

There are many of the teachings of Jesus which are about living and working together. Let us read two of them. As you read pay particular attention to see if the way people think or behave made any difference in Jesus' feelings toward them. Matthew 5:43-48; 7:12.

Role Playing. The group may divide into small committees and role play Christian solutions to some problems in everyday living. Role playing means to assume the part of the characters in the problem and try to work out a solution to the problem in keeping with that person's feelings and background. The problems should illustrate situations where people are different or where there are differences in opinion. There may have been situations which arose in the group itself that can be remembered and discussed without embarrassment to any member of the group. Various ways of working out a solution may be shown in the role playing. Some possible problems are described below if it is not possible to use actual situations from the group itself.

1. A new boy or girl comes to camp. This person is wearing clothing and speaking in a way that is quite different from the other members of the group.

2. John does not want to include the girls in a game of dodge ball. Mary does not think this is fair.

3. Ann whispers uncomplimentary remarks to other members of the group about Susan. Susan has not yet learned to handle her knife and fork properly when eating meat.

4. Bill thinks that farmers and dairymen and those who produce food are by far the most important people in the world. Tom does not agree. He thinks those who produce the machinery and trucks and equipment for such work are more important.

WORSHIP

Each member of the group may choose a favorite passage from the Bible, a poem, a story, or a hymn to be shared with the entire group. Counselors may give guidance where necessary. The prayer may be one of appreciation for the great variety in our world, for the freedom we have of choosing, and for an understanding of those whose opinions are different from ours.

I MAKE MY CONTRIBUTION

DISCUSSION AREAS

How a simple act or contribution can sometimes be very important to a whole group of people.

Each person has a responsibility for making this contribution.

Story. Many years ago when our country was very young and much of it was an unknown wilderness, there lived a man whose name was John Chapman. He noticed that the settlers were moving farther and farther west into the wilderness of the Allegheny Mountains. He thought about the hardships these people would have in finding food and shelter in a strange, unknown wilderness and wanted to help.

He visited the cider mills in the settled regions of Pennsylvania. There he saw thousands of seeds that had been dumped out with the pulp after the juice had been taken from the apples. He gathered together all the seeds he could carry.

With his seeds he rowed up the tributaries of the Ohio River. Always he watched for open spaces in the forest. When he saw such a space, he stopped to plant some of his apple seeds. After the seeds were planted, he wove a strong brush fence to go all around the open space. This fence kept the deer from eating the tender shoots of the young trees.

On John Chapman went until he had planted many beds of seeds. He revisited the nurseries he had started and chose strong and sturdy seedlings for transplanting. If for some reason his first seeds had not grown, he planted more. Sometimes deer broke through the brush fence or damaged it trying to get to the young, tender leaves. John Chapman repaired the fences and moved on to another nursery.

Each year he moved farther into the wilderness planting and tending his nurseries so that the settlers might find apple trees growing when they arrived. As the settlers discovered the trees and learned who had planted and cared for them, they loved John Chapman. They named him "Johnny Appleseed."

DISCUSSION

Almost anyone can plant seeds and care for them. That is simple and easy work. Why was it such an important activity for the early settlers?

Do you know workmen whose work makes life easier and happier for others—local doctors, nurses, ministers, dairymen, grocerymen, teachers, bakers, and so on? Are all these professions needed in our world? What would happen if every person chose to be a doctor; or a dairyman; or a baker; or a minister? What are some questions a person should ask himself when he is ready to choose a profession?

Each plant and each animal in the world makes a contribution. Many of these contributions can be used for the good of mankind. Some contributions are small, such as a drop of nectar a bee finds in a single flower; but they are important. The more knowledge we have about the world, the more we realize God's great wisdom in planning it.

God planned for every flower, every blade of grass, every insect and every animal. Each one makes some contribution. Not all these contributions are known but each year we learn more about the world and the part each plant and animal has in it.

Do you think God has planned so carefully for the plants and animals and has not planned for boys and girls, men and women? Scientists who have studied the universe have found that God planned an orderly world that could keep itself in perfect balance. Do you think God also planned a way for boys and girls, and men and women to keep a perfect balance as they live and work together?

Think about your friends. Can they do activities that you cannot do? Do they have abilities like good singing voices or skill in drawing that you do not have? Name some skills and abilities your friends have that you do not have.

You have abilities, too. There are activities which you can do. You may not be able to do all that your friends can do, but you can do, or can learn to do, many activities. Think about yourself. What have you already learned to do? What would you like to learn to do? Why have you not learned to do this particular activity?

There is much helpful guidance in the Bible about living and working as Christians. In the New Testament there is a verse which says, "Do not neglect to do good and to share what you have." (Hebrews 13:16.) How are we living this verse here in camp? Let us each answer for ourself how we may better live this verse.

Paul was a very important person to the early Christian church. He wrote much helpful guidance about living and working together as Christians. He must have believed that God planned a world where each person has a contribution to make. At least he was interested in each doing his best. He wrote to the Christians at Colossae, "Whatever your task, work heartily." (Colossians 3:23.)

The section in the camper's book titled, "Here's to You—the Camper Enjoys Stories," may be used with this discussion.

WORSHIP

The group may work out a worship service of their own. This is a very fine opportunity to help them work out a service in which each member of the group may make a contribution. It should not be a series of scriptural readings or poetry but a well-planned and organized service using as many aids to worship as are meaningful.

The counselors will remember that we all worship best through the use of the familiar. The experiences of the group, the hymns they know, the scripture that has come to have meaning for them, a poem that has inspired them to worship, or a story that has worship value will more nearly lead to a real experience of worship than all new materials.

67

DISCUSSION AREAS

Difficulties faced by plants in trying to make their contribution to the world.

Difficulties faced by persons as they try to make their contribution.

How people may be helped in making their contribution.

DISCUSSION

Sometimes a tree in the forest has a difficult time manufacturing its own food. Do you know what causes such difficulties for a tree? Other trees may be growing so close around that its leaves are shaded from the sun. The larger root systems of other trees may absorb the water from the soil. The tree is hindered in making its contribution to the world because of the other trees around it.

Have you seen flower beds that were too full of plants? What happens to the plants? What can be done to help each plant to grow and bloom? Each one needs a chance to grow.

There are persons who have difficulty in making their contribution. Sometimes a person feels like that tree in the forest. Those around seem so big and so important that he becomes shy and timid. Are those around more important? Does this person have a contribution to make, too?

What can we do for a shy or timid person? Does teasing help? How does teasing make such a person feel? Does laughing at him help? How does that make one feel? Do you think a friendly smile would help? Why do you think so? How about a word of encouragement? If a shy or timid person tries and does not do too well, should we say, "Aw, that's no good!" or, "You can do better next time"? Why do you think so?

Sometimes boys and girls work so close together that everyone does not have room. Have you seen that happen? Do they do their best work when crowded? Sometimes in our conversation some of us talk so hard and fast that others are crowded out. Have you known of that happening? What can be done about such behavior?

There are those who need to learn happy ways of working together. Most of us are in this group. We need to work without saying words or acting in a way that hurts or irritates. We need to learn to encourage and help those who have difficulty in making their contribution. How can we help one another to learn?

Jesus believed that every person was important. Again and again, he helped people by showing them that God loves each individual and wants him to be happy.

One day when Jesus was talking with the people, he called their attention to the birds and lilies. He talked about God's care for them. Matthew 6:26-31.

In what ways does God care for the birds? Did Jesus feel that people were of more value to God than birds? What does Jesus say about the lilies? How has God cared for them? How does Jesus show that people are more important than flowers?

There is another story from the New Testament of Jesus' teaching about the importance of people to God. Read Matthew 10:29-31. How does he try here to help people understand their importance?

WORSHIP

The group may recall some of their experiences as a group with particular attention to the contributions that have been made by the individual campers. Be very careful that something good is mentioned about the contribution of each member of the group and that the compliments are sincere.

Out of this sharing there should come some real appreciations for the individual members of the group and of their abilities. The group might compose a litany of thanks for helpers in this world, for members of the group, and for God's love that helps each one of us to feel that he is important and that he can do his part.

The hymn "The World One Neighborhood" may be sung. (See camper's book, page 27.) Special attention may be given to the lines which speak of "one another's good."

I WORK WITH OTHERS IN MY CHURCH

DISCUSSION AREAS
What is a church?
What is the work of the church?
Who helps the church carry on its work?
How can I help?

DISCUSSION

There are many kinds of church buildings in the world. Some are great, beautiful buildings. Others are not so large and are more simple. Still others are small. There are church buildings with only one room. What do you like about the building in which your church meets?

What really makes a church important? Is it the minister? Is it the building? Is it the people? If we think about the work of the church it will help us discover the answer to this question.

There are many activities in a church building all through the year. Can you think of those in your church? Do you have church school sessions each Sunday; how about vacation church school in the summer; times of worship? Does it take time and work to have these activities? Does it take money?

Why do you think the people of your church take the time, spend the money, and do the work necessary for all of these activities? It is through such activities that people learn about Jesus and what he taught about God. It is in this way that they learn happy ways of living and working together.

The people who make up the church are also interested in all who live in the community. How does your community help those who need food and clothing? Do you have a Community Chest or United Givers' Fund? How does it help those who have needs? From where does the money for this work come?

How are those who are sick cared for in your community? Do you know a doctor or a nurse who is a member of your church's congregation? Have you ever been in a hospital in your community? Do you know some of the ways a hospital helps a community? Sometimes hospitals are built by special groups of people because they want to help a community stay well and healthy. Many hospitals are built and operated by churches.

In many communities there are centers built especially to minister to those who need friendliness and love. Do you know persons in your church who work in such a center? Many persons give money to help with this work. They give their money through the church. Sometimes, one church group will build and support such a center.

There are many groups in most communities who are trying to show lovingkindness to all who need it. These groups may be called by various names but all of them were started by people with a Christian concern for others. All Christian people should be concerned about helping and loving others.

Could a church carry on its work without people? Why? How do the people help? Are there ways in which boys and girls can help, too? Would the church be able to do as much if only a few gave money or helped in some other way? It takes many people working together for the church to carry on all its work.

The people of a church are not only interested in their own community. They are interested in people everywhere who need love and care. Do you know how the church is helping in other parts of our country; of the world? It takes many people and many churches working together to carry on all these activities. Why do you think the church is a good example of people working together?

Worship

Stories from the early church such as those found in Acts 4:32-35 and 11:27-30 may be told or read from the Bible and discussed. A prayer of thanksgiving for the church and what it has meant to people through the centuries might close this time of worship.

70

The process of preparing a meal outdoors makes us all more aware of how far mankind has advanced in learning to make daily living easier.

Frying bacon on a hobo stove makes prominent the efficiency of an electric stove in a modern kitchen. Gathering wood and building a fire for cooking make one conscious of man's ingeniousness in harnessing water power or natural gas to produce instant heat for any kind of cooking. Such appreciations are the bases for expressions of gratitude for God's gifts of mental ingenuity that have helped men develop all these skills.

When campers have shared responsibilities and worked together for the good of all, attitudes of friendliness and genuine appreciation for one another are developed. There is an awareness of the interdependence of all, for it has been exemplified in the activity of a cook-out. This is God's plan for his children—that they learn ways of working happily together, each concerned about the others. After such an experience it is a natural step to give thanks for God's plan and for our part in it, with a petition that we continue to learn and practice happy ways of working together.

Grace for an outdoor meal can be a lovely and worshipful experience. Out of this working together there grows a spirit of group fellowship that opens the door for worship. A grace that includes the entire group can catch the spirit of fellowship better and lift it into worship. It may be a litany of thanks, a musical grace, or one that is well enough known by the group to be said in unison. Musical graces should be learned in advance. It is not wise to learn a musical grace at the time it is to be used for worship. Its very newness takes away from the freedom and ease a group needs in their expressions of gratitude to God for his goodness. The same may be said for spoken graces. Sometimes the group may write or compose their own grace to be said in unison. The following litany is an example of a type of grace that can be very meaningful and provides an opportunity for everyone to participate.

> For wind and sun and rain and soil that make the food grow,
>> We thank you, God.
> For friends working together to grow and cook and serve the food,
>> We thank you, God.
> For the joy of planning and working and eating together,
>> We thank you, God. Amen.

Many times in such an experience of cooking and eating out of doors there is an opportunity to discuss the processes of this universe that make living possible and pleasant. Some biblical materials, such as the following selections from Psalms 65 and 104, will help the group find expression for their feelings.

71

Thou visitest the earth and waterest it,
    thou greatly enrichest it;
the river of God is full of water;
    thou providest their grain,
    for so thou hast prepared it.
Thou waterest its furrows abundantly,
    settling its ridges,
softening it with showers,
    and blessing its growth.
Thou crownest the year with thy bounty;
    the tracks of thy chariot drip with fatness.
The pastures of the wilderness drip,
    the hills gird themselves with joy,
the meadows clothe themselves with flocks,
    the valleys deck themselves with grain,
    they shout and sing together for joy.

. . . .

Thou makest springs gush forth in the valleys;
    they flow between the hills,
they give drink to every beast of the field;

. . . .

By them the birds of the air have their habitation;
    they sing among the branches.
From thy lofty abode thou waterest the mountains;
    the earth is satisfied with the fruit of thy work.
Thou dost cause the grass to grow for the cattle,
    and plants for man to cultivate,
that he may bring forth food from the earth, . . .
oil to make his face shine,
    and bread to strengthen man's heart.

—Psalms 65:9-13; 104:10-15

5

David enjoys a special day

David giggled as he joined the group under the pine tree. "Sure is funny to go swimming in the woods," he said.

Everyone laughed at David's remark. They did look funny to each other all dressed in their bathing suits for a walk along the trail.

"Good way to spend a rainy morning," Ray said, counting to be sure everyone was present. "Come on, let's go. Everyone is here."

Down the trail they went splashing through the puddles and enjoying the feel of the soft earth under their sneakers. The raindrops splashed against their bodies. It was a new experience for David. He liked the cool, wet rain falling on his back. It felt as if he were taking a cold shower with the water running very slowly.

Ray held up his hand for everyone to stop. "Listen to the drip, drip of the rain on the leaves over our heads," he said.

It sounded as if there were great drops of water being thrown against the leaves one at a time. David watched big drops running together to make even bigger ones on the witch hazel leaves just off the trail.

"Wow!" Tom broke the silence with a big whoop. "Listen, nothing!" he cried. "A great big one hit me right on the ear. Let's get moving." Everyone laughed at Tom trying to dry his ear, with the rain wetting it again faster than he could dry it off.

It was cool and damp in the woods now. There was a fresh, clean smell along the trail which David liked very much. It was not long until they

were walking alongside the lake. Everyone paused to watch the raindrops hitting the surface of the water.

"Bounces like a ball," Carol said quietly.

"And the circles run into each other trying to get to the shore," Mirian answered.

"Time to get back to camp and get on warm dry clothes," Betty called from up front. "Run up the hill in a hurry."

It was a breathless group of campers that shortly came out on top of the knoll. Under the tarps everyone put on warm dry clothing. Wet bathing suits were hung on a clothesline out in the rain.

"I like the woods in the rain," David was saying to Ray when they heard Betty's voice calling from the girls' tarp.

"Come on over," she said. "We are ready."

When the boys arrived they found the girls all seated around a box marked "Rainy Day Chest." They were begging Betty to tell them what was inside. "Wait and see," Betty said with a knowing smile. "Wait and see."

"Here we go," Ray said, seating himself in front of the box. "David, where's your knife? Cut the tape."

David cut the tape that held the lid on the box. Everyone moved forward as Ray lifted the lid. Ten pairs of eager eyes were gazing down to see what treasures were in the chest.

"Oh, boy."

"Hot ziggety."

"Look at that!"

"I see what I want!"

There was a whole chorus of remarks. Out came puzzles, clay, wood for carving, books, enough for everyone. It was not long until there was a busy, happy hum under the tarp.

David looked around the group. Tom and Cavin were trying to work a puzzle. Ray, Mirian, Carol, and John were whittling away with some balsa wood. There was a whole group around Betty making pins to take home as gifts. "Camp sure is fun," he thought, picking up the new book he wanted to read. "Even on a rainy day."

SPECIAL DAYS AT CAMP

Certain days in camp are labeled "special days," not because they are important on the calendar, but because of their importance to the spirit and purpose of the camp. Ray and Betty made a rainy day a special one because they had anticipated its coming and made preparation for it. Some days that may be "special" are listed here and suggestions given for keeping them as such.

OPENING DAY

The first day at camp is a very important one. This is the camper's first impression of the camp situation, and for the sake of all concerned it should be good. The counselors should make careful preparation for helping each camper to feel welcome and happy from the beginning in spite of any unexpected difficulties that may arise. Even a rainy day for opening need not dampen spirits of campers.

Making a name tag is always a fascinating activity for a camper. This is a good "first experience." Various kinds of materials may be on hand and each camper can choose the kind he wants to make. Suggestions for name tags are given in the section on activities. The campers have probably been looking forward for a long time to the experience of camp. The sooner they get into a real camp activity the more comfortable and satisfied they will be. They may discover the bounds of the camp and some of the interesting sights around the area.

This trip might include a visit to the swimming area. This would be a good opportunity to meet the water front director and to talk with him about swimming regulations. They may even work out a time for the first swim period.

A visit to the camp nurse is also a good experience for the first day in camp. They may learn what to do in case of injury or when in need of insect repellent or any of the other small remedies so often needed in camp. They may check out the first-aid kit for their group on this visit. The nurse may explain the contents and their use.

If there are certain dangers around the camp such as poison ivy or areas to be avoided for one reason or another this is a good time to learn about them. These should be discussed last. It can be a bit discouraging to be greeted with a list of "noes" immediately upon arrival at camp!

There may be a time of group games to help the campers get acquainted with one another on this opening day. Group singing also helps to give a feeling of unity and good fellowship. The small groups may begin to make some plans of their own as to how they would like to spend their days at camp.

RAINY DAYS

Usually there is at least one rainy day during the period of time covered by a camp, and sometimes more. Unless rainy days have been anticipated and some preparation made, they can be disastrous. However, if plans are made for rainy days they can be most enjoyable.

A group of juniors will thoroughly enjoy a walk or romp out in a warm summer rain. It is fun to feel the patter of rain against the body. The campers may wear bathing suits and shower or bathing caps. They should not stay out too long and should change into warm dry clothing immediately upon their return.

A "Rainy Day Chest" may be prepared before camp opens. This may be a large box filled with quiet games, puzzles, story books, craft materials, and song books. The box is sealed and may be painted to represent an old treasure chest. It should remain mysteriously sealed until a rainy day arrives. Then it is opened. Each takes a turn at enjoying its contents.

If the day is cool, an open fireplace in a resident camp and a good storyteller or a book of adventure stories well read can turn an otherwise dreary day into a glorious adventure. Every counselor should bring to camp one or more such story books.

Some resident camps have a lodge that can be used for indoor games and activities on a rainy day. Such games as checkers, Ping-pong, jackstones, Chinese checkers, and so on are provided. These games may be interspersed with such crafts as wood carving, weaving, and clay modeling. There may also be periods of storytelling and group singing.

The group may learn the song "Rain Music" found in *Singing Worship*. The latter part of Psalms 65 may be read, discussed and learned as a choral reading.

There are several recordings of music that have been written to describe rain. If there is some place around camp where a record player can be set up these recordings may be interpreted and enjoyed. Some of these recordings are:

Cloudburst by Grofé, from *Grand Canyon Suite* (Victor Album LM 1928, 33—1/3 rpm).

The Storm by Rossini, from Overture to William Tell (Victor Album LM 1986, 33—1/3 rpm).

Prelude Op. 28, No. 15 by Chopin, which Liszt called "Raindrop Prelude" (Victor Album LM 1168, 33—1/3 rpm). Campers may listen to discover why he so named it.

SUNDAY

Resident camps that are ten days to two weeks in length will have at least one Sunday in camp. Some decisions will need to be made by the director and counselors about this day before camp opens.

The Old Testament concept of the Sabbath was a day of rest and was therefore accompanied by a cessation from all labor. Elaborate rules and laws and regulations were brought into effect to see that this purpose was accomplished.

Jesus' concept was that the Sabbath was a day of reviving the body through relaxation and the spirit through praise and thanksgiving and worship. He said, "The sabbath was made for man, not man for the sabbath" (Mark 2:27).

Almost every generation has observed some special taboo or custom with regard to the day that is kept for worship and relaxation. Thus it may become a day for dissension and tension if these taboos and customs are enforced on all members of the group without their participation in making the decision. Certainly no director or counselor wants this sort of observance of Sunday in camp. Therefore it will be wise to talk through, before camp opens, the policy for observing Sunday. Then everyone will have an understanding of the attitude that is to be taken.

Sunday will be a special day in camp. Since there may be more leisure time on this day, some extra sleep in the morning will help refresh tired bodies. Something special for breakfast will help to create the atmosphere of a special day.

The worship service for the day may come early in the morning before the heat rises or may be in the late afternoon. This worship service might well be built around the experiences of the week that has just passed. Hymns, scriptural passages, choral readings, stories, and dramatizations that have helped in group worship during the week may be worked into this service. If an offering is taken, it may go to some special project chosen by the group.

The groups may spend part of the day enjoying such activities as listening to music, singing, writing cards and notes, telling stories, strolling along woodland trails. If there is something they have particularly enjoyed, they may share it with another group.

The evening meal may be a bag lunch or a cook-out in order to give the kitchen staff some free time for relaxation and rest. This is a good time for fellowship singing, sharing stories, and playing games.

CLOSING DAY

Closing day is a very important one in camp. It should be the climax of the total experience and should be just as rich and meaningful as any other day.

Good campers leave their outdoor camp site clean and cleared as far as possible of all evidence of their having camped there. Tarpaulins or other shelters should be taken down and stored away. All tools should be returned to their proper places. Any equipment should be put safely away for another group using the site that year, or until another year.

Children learn through evaluating their experiences and relating them to their everyday lives. There should be some time on this closing day for the campers to evaluate their experiences. This may be done in their camp site after it has been cleaned or in a favorite spot along the trail or in the woods. A good outline for such an evaluation is:

1. What has been good about our days in camp?

2. At what points did we fail to do our best? How could we have improved?

3. How can we put into practice in our homes and communities what we have learned at camp about living and working happily with others?

This evaluation may be followed by a prayer of thanksgiving in which the campers give thanks for those experiences they have especially enjoyed. They may also ask God's help for continuing to practice Christian habits of happy group living.

The discovery group may visit a favorite spot again. They may enjoy some games and songs they have especially liked.

The Constant Star [1]

Of course, Pavlos should not have forgotten for one small minute that he was a goatherd. It was especially important that he prove himself trustworthy because his widowed mother depended on the little money he earned tending the flocks of his Turkish neighbor, Zia Effendi. He should have kept his eyes on the goats every minute of every day—but just once he forgot.

It had been a long time since he had eaten his lunch of hard dark bread and pale white cheese. He followed the goats under a wild apple tree, bowed down with the ripe, red fruit. Every boy knows that the apples at the top of a tree seem sweetest. Up the tree went Pavlos. Apple after apple he munched. He swung his legs contentedly, and, just for a moment, completely forgot that he was a goatherd.

"Oh, the goats!" Pavlos remembered with a start. He slid down the tree, making a new tear for his patient mother to patch. "Where are they?"

Not a goat was in sight!

Pavlos ran wildly over the hills, calling. He stood still holding his breath, to listen. Not the switch of a woolly tail! Not the tinkle of a little brass bell!

"They must have gone home by themselves!" Pavlos looked at the glow where the sun had just slipped behind the mountain. "It's after the time we usually start. They ought to know the way home."

Pavlos ran down the hilly trail toward the village. Each time that he rounded a boulder or mounted a hilltop to gain a new view of the trail in the gathering dusk, he hoped for the sight of his flock. "They must be beyond the next rise of ground," he would say as he ran on.

"They must be in their own fold," he said when he reached the last hilltop above his village. It was almost dark now, but the white of the goats would have been visible, had they been on the path. "I hope Zia Effendi will not be cross that they come alone."

But Zia Effendi was cross—not because the goats had come home alone but because they had not come home at all.

"They must be here," said Pavlos. "They were nowhere on the hills. I would have heard their bells tinkling even if I could not see them."

"Back to the hills, young man, and find those goats!" ordered Zia Effendi.

---

[1] From *Stories for Junior Worship*. Copyright 1941 by Whitmore & Stone. Used by permission of Abingdon Press.

"It is dark," Pavlos shivered as he gazed at the hills rising so blackly. "Let me go for them in the morning. They will be all right."

"All right alone on those hills?" Effendi laughed mockingly. "Do you hear that noise?"

Pavlos heard and shivered. It was the howl of a jackal far off on the hillside.

Zia Effendi began telling what the jackals would do to a flock of defenseless goats. Pavlos was thinking what those same jackels would do to one small boy.

"Go back to the hills and find those goats!" There was no arguing with Zia Effendi when he spoke like that.

Suddenly Pavlos felt an arm about him.

"I wish I could go with you." It was his mother's voice. "But I cannot leave your little brother while he is sick. Here is bread and cheese to eat on the way. Keep saying the prayer 'Our Father' that we say in church every Sunday. The Father will keep you safe."

Pavlos took the food, gave his mother a hug, and started off into the blackness. It was so much darker going away from home than it had been walking toward the lights of the home village. Only the stars were with him—and the jackals.

He had heard the jackals howl at night when he played with the village boys, but he had never realized before how threatening were their voices. His legs felt as limp as the macaroni cooked in his mother's big copper kettle. On he went, stumbling over rocks and brambles. Round and round the hilltop he wandered. He had lost all sense of direction. All he knew was that somewhere on the hills were the goats, and that he must find them before the jackals did. He tried to hush his own wheezing breath so that he could hear the tinkle of a little brass bell, if one of the goats should stir. They must be asleep now, sleeping so soundly that there would be no tinkling. He realized now that they had probably gone to sleep before he had given up hunting them. The sound that never ceased was the howling of the jackals. It seemed to come nearer and nearer.

"It is growing late." Pavlos talked out loud to keep himself company. "I can tell from the position of the Great Dipper. It is not where it is in early evening."

Pavlos tried to remember the prayer his mother had told him to say, but his mind was so numb with fear and weariness that the words would not come. Nor would any other words of comfort.

He stumbled over a rock and sat where he fell—too tired and discouraged to wander farther. Suddenly, just over a big rock from him, came the sweetest sound he had ever heard—the tinkle of a little brass bell. Feeling his way carefully, he rounded the rock and found the sleeping goats huddled close together. One of them was scratching his ear with his hind leg, making that blessed tinkle.

Pavlos threw himself into the middle of the flock, patting the goats, counting them, crying tears of relief into their warm silky coats.

"Every goat is here!"

The jackals on the hillside howled, but they did not seem so near nor so terrifying now that Pavlos was no longer alone.

"Wake up, my good goats!" called Pavlos. "We must go home."

The goats staggered sleepily to their feet and stood about Pavlos, waiting to be led. The boy turned slowly round and round. On every side was blackness. The lights of his home village lay hidden behind some hills. But in which direction? He looked this way and that way, but the darkness seemed alike on all sides. He knew that the village was north of the hills where he was standing. But which way was north? The night was growing late. He could tell by the way the Great Dipper had swung along its nightly journey about Polaris, the North Star.

"The North Star!" Pavlos fairly shouted this name to the black hills and the drowsy goats and the howling jackals. "The North Star never seems to move. It will lead me home. It is always in the north."

Pavlos gathered the goats about him and followed the star, "the constant star that guides men by its light." It was hard walking and slow, but not for one moment did Pavlos feel lost. The planets might take their wandering path among the stars, and the constellations might take their nightly swing about the North Star, but the one fixed star would guide him home.

At last the few lights still burning in the village came into view. As Pavlos gave a last look at the guiding star, the words of the prayer his mother had urged him to say flashed back into his mind, "Our Father which art in heaven, Hallowed be thy name . . . for thine is the kingdom and the power, and the glory forever."

Pavlos, gazing up at the stars, added a prayer of his own, "Our Father, who made the stars obey your laws, I thank you."

A Bird in His Hand [2]

Steve slid from his bicycle and leaned it against the iron railing of the bridge over Curving Creek. He wiggled free from his newspaper bag and stuffed it in the carrier of his bicycle. He buttoned the flap to his pocket to be sure his change purse was safe. Then he climbed over the old stone fence and dug his heels into the soft soil of the steep bank leading down to Curving Creek.

---

[2] By Alice Geer Kelsey. From *Trails for Juniors.* Copyright 1951 by Pierce and Smith. Used by permission.

"Last time I came down here the ground was frozen," he thought aloud.

He leaped and scrambled and slid down to the creek's edge. Water rippled freely where it had gurgled under a glaze of ice only a few days ago.

Steve plunged his way through the thick growth of alders at the water's edge, looking for the fluff of gray on the pussy willows. It was there, waiting to push into soft gray balls on the first warm days.

"Too early for hepaticas," he thought. But he could not resist looking at the place where he found them each spring. He saw only the brown dead leaves which had been there all winter, snow-covered.

Steve jumped from rock to rock across the brook and squashed into the swamp. He stooped beside a cluster of firm, coppery-red tips. "I thought you would begin peeking out about now," he said to the very young points of skunks' cabbage. "I do not care if you do smell like your name. You have lots more courage than some flowers that smell sweeter. They come along when you have already stuck your nose out of the ground to prove that spring is on the way."

Steve slogged out of the swamp, leaped across his steppingstones, forced his way through the alders, pulling himself up the bank and rolled over the old stone fence. He jumped onto his bicycle and was off to deliver the rest of his papers.

This was the day of the week when his route took most time, even without stopping at Curving Creek. This was the day he had to collect twenty-four cents from each customer. At most houses this stop was just business, leaning against the wall while women tried to remember in which bag they had used their coin purses last. At other houses it grew into a friendly call.

The Matthews' house was one where Steve sometimes stayed longer than he planned. Though the Matthews boys were grown and away from home, their mother had not forgotten how to talk with boys. Things that would have meant little at any other house on his route grew exciting when she talked about them.

Today she was opening a box which had just arrived in the mail. She had that shining look of something-going-to-happen. "I hope it is as lovely as I remember it," she said as she pried the top of the carton open. Steve hoped so, too, and waited to see what it could be.

He watched her pull out crumple after crumple of protecting newspapers, then something wrapped in roll after roll of corrugated cardboard.

"When I saw it in the store it made me feel like thanking God for all outdoor goodness and beauty." She peeled away layer after layer of wrapping. "That is how I hope people will feel when they look at my flower arrangement at the Flower Show."

She laughed with Steve at herself for sounding so sure about winning a place in the Flower Show. Steve knew that almost every woman on his route was planning a flower arrangement. He knew that only two or three of the very best would be chosen at the local show to be entered in the great Flower Show in the big city. Of course, he hoped that Mrs. Matthews would be one of the winners.

The last wrapping fell away. Mrs. Matthews held up a silver-gray statue about as long as Steve's arm. It showed a young man in a monk's gown. In his hand he held a bird, and the bird looked glad to be there. The young man's face was lifted heavenward with a smile of peace on it. He seemed to be joining God in loving birds and flowers and people and all growing things.

"Oh-h!" said Steve. "Who is he?"

"Saint Francis of Assisi," said Mrs. Matthews. "He was a rich young man who lived in Italy about seven hundred years ago. He gave up all his wealth in order to spend his life helping people. He called himself the little brother of the poor. To him all growing things were brothers and sisters."

"I've heard his name," said Steve, "but I don't know much about him. I'd like to know, though."

"There are two books about him there on the table," she said. "The one in plain gray binding was written hundreds of years ago by people who lived when Saint Francis did, or a few years later. The one with bright-colored pictures puts those stories into words boys and girls of today can enjoy. You may take it home to read if you wish."

Steve picked up the book and looked at its pictures of the slim gray-clad monk with the joyous face. This Saint Francis of Assisi must have been a *doing* sort of person. Each picture promised a lively story. He was buying a caged bird in the market place to set it free. He was taming a fierce wolf by mere kindness. He was giving food to thieves who had tried to rob the monastery where he lived. He was talking to hundreds of birds who were twittering about him as though they were all talking together. He was braving the savage power of the great sultan of the East who had vowed the death of every Christian who crossed his path. Always there was a bird in his hand.

"Thanks!" Steve tucked the book into his newspaper bag.

Next week found Mrs. Matthews working at her table beside the silver gray statue. Beside her was a big box of assorted flowers from the florist.

"Lucky I have twenty-four cents left to pay you," laughed Mrs. Matthews. "I had to buy these flowers to practice arranging them around Saint Francis. Then I'll know just what flowers to buy fresh for our local competition, and I suppose if I place, I'll have to buy flowers again for the arrangement at the Flower Show in the big city."

Steve stood close to her as she tried the flowers in different vases, in different positions. He listened as she talked about what was important in flower arrangement—about color, design, meaning. Then, because she was a mother of boys, she said, "What do you think of it."

"Do you really want me to tell you?"

"Of course!" Mrs. Matthews was surprised at something new in his voice.

"I have been reading your book about Saint Francis," Steve began. "I think I know him pretty well now. I think I know what he would say about your flowers."

"Tell me!"

Steve hesitated.

"It will be Saint Francis saying it," Mrs. Matthews encouraged him. "It won't be Steve Robinson talking."

That made it easier. Steve drew himself tall and threw his head back. As he had lived every word of the book, it was easy for him to live Saint Francis now.

"Sister Matthews," he said, "do you forget that I am the little brother of the poor? If I had money, I would buy bread and shoes for the hungry and the cold. I would not buy rare flowers grown out of their seasons. I am not happy among these expensive flowers. I am at home among the common things of the field and woods—with a bird in my hand."

"A fine speech, my young saint," laughed Mrs. Matthews, "and true. But tell me, you wise one of Assisi, what 'common things of field and woods' can I find in bloom at this time of year?"

Steve laughed and started for the door. With his hand on the door-knob he asked, "Have you explored Curving Creek yet this spring?"

"Curving Creek? I have not been closer than the bridge since my boys used to go wading there years ago."

Next collecting day, Steve once more found Mrs. Matthews at work beside the statue of Saint Francis. This time there was no florist's box on the table. Instead there was a pack basket on the floor. Steve took one long look at what she was doing and whistled.

"You've been to Curving Creek!" he cried.

"Every day and twice on Sunday," she agreed. "What would Saint Francis say of my flower arrangement now?"

"Sister Matthews!" Steve went into his Saint Francis act. "You have made me feel at home among the common things of the creek bank. That old stump, water washed and weather beaten, curves upward with my thoughts. The reeds against the stump remind me of the birds who would swing on them as they sing their songs of springtime. The catkins of the alder and the gray of the pussy willow. Shucks, I can't talk fast enough that way. It's swell, Mrs. Matthews. It's the plain outdoors that fits with Saint Francis' statue."

"One question, Steve," she asked. "Do you suppose a spray of yellow forsythia would be out of place among the alders and the pussy willows? There should be a touch of brighter color. I am forcing forsythia branches picked from the bush under the window."

"I think Francis of Assisi would like the yellow." Steve was studying the sweeping upward curves of the budded sprays. "It would remind him of his brother Sun."

"Another thing. Good flower arrangement demands something rich toned and low growing between the statue and the branches." Mrs. Matthews pointed at the bare spot. "I cannot find a thing that is right."

Steve studied the blank spot. He laughed as an idea struck him. "Saint Francis liked very common things, didn't he?" said Steve.

"He loved every growing thing, no matter how common."

"He loved them even if they were not sweet smelling like roses or arbutus, didn't he?"

"I'm sure he did."

"I have only two more papers to deliver," said Steve, picking up his bag. "Then I'll go to the bank of Curving Creek that was too wet for you to reach. I'll be back soon."

Half an hour later Mrs. Matthews was at the door when Steve rode up quite out of breath. His bicycle carrier was full of something glossy and coppery-red.

"Oh, what a smell!" exclaimed Mrs. Matthews as she welcomed him into the house, muddy shoes and all. "I have not smelled skunks' cabbage since the boys and I used to cross Curving Creek on the rocks. I had forgotten how sturdy and shining the young plants are. What a rich color! Quick! Let's see how they look!"

Carefully she spaced three coppery-red skunks' cabbages on the flat part of the gray stump, between the silver-gray Francis of Assisi and the upward curving branches. Then they stood back to admire.

"Just the right color!" said she.

"Just the right size!" said he.

"Just the right commonness," they said as though they thought of it at the same instant.

Later, at the Flower Show in the great city, some people wondered why a freckled-faced boy with country mud on his shoes sat entranced before the niche where a silver-gray Saint Francis with a bird in his hand looked upward while an arrangement of stumps, reeds, and flowering branches pointed upward also.

Steve smiled to hear some city people wondering what the rare coppery-red plant at the base of the stump might be. It seemed to Steve that the statue smiled with him. Steve and Saint Francis knew that there was goodness and beauty in the commonest of God's growing things.

On the Shores of the Aegean [3]

This imaginary story of a Greek slave boy who found a friend in the apostle John on the Isle of Patmos points out how those who have seemingly wronged us may love and forgive.

I. THE BOY SLAVE

Day after day, month after month, Jason, the Greek slave, had dreamed a great dream of the time when he should win fame and freedom.

It would be the day of the foot race in the Olympian games, and he would be in the race, the Marathon race, which made the Greeks remember how their country had once saved its liberties from the invading Persians.

For nearly eight hundred years the games at Olympia had been part of the life of the people of Greece. Greek cities, fighting one another had even halted wars so that the games might be held. Greece was no longer a free nation. Rome ruled the World, but the games at Olympia, in Elis, in the deep valley of Alpheus, still went on.

Once every four years young men and boys from all over Greece met near the sacred grove beside the river Alpheus. There they tried their skill in wrestling, in jumping, in running, in boxing, in driving chariots. There the winners were given prizes, wreaths of wild olive from the sacred grove. The crowds cheered them; and, when they went home, their cities honored them.

Greater than any event was the foot race, a long-distance running race. It made the Greeks remember how the runner from Marathon had saved Athens from the Persians. It was the race which Jason hoped to win.

For two years he had been training for it. The governor of Patmos had sent for Jason one day after the boy had been running on the beach with the governor's son, Marcus. "You are to go to Elis." he told Jason. "You are to go with my son."

"To the games?" Jason cried. "To the Olympian games?"

"To the games," the governor said.

For two years Jason had believed that he, with Marcus, was to enter the foot race. Dreaming, he had seen himself the winner, had heard the shouts of the crowd, had pictured his glorious return, had even planned how the governor would give freedom to him. He would live a freeman. The victor at Olympia could be given nothing less than freedom.

Now, crushed and miserable, the boy sat on the high rock which looked out on the sea. His dream was dead. For today Marcus had told him the truth. Jason was to go to Elis with him, but Jason could not run in the

[3] By Dr. Mary Synon. From *This Is Our Heritage.* Faith and Freedom Readers, Book VI. Used by permission of Commission on American Citizenship of the Catholic University of America in Washington, D.C., and Ginn and Company, Publishers.

race. Only freemen, children of freemen, could enter the games; and Jason was a slave.

"I hate Marcus now as much as I once loved him," the boy told himself, as he stared down on the beach where he and Marcus had so often raced together. "He has known, all this time, that I could not go into the race at Elis, but he has kept me from knowing it so that I might help him to win. But I will find a way to keep him from winning. If I cannot win, neither shall he!"

Jason was still deep in the bitterness of his disappointment when he saw Marcus come upon the beach below. The son of the governor, looking up at a soaring bird, saw Jason on the rocks. "Come on!" he cried. From the tone of his voice Jason thought that Marcus was making fun of him. "Come on!" Marcus repeated.

Instantly Jason was on his feet. With unbelievable swiftness he sprang down the cliff until he stood beside Marcus. "You cannot do this to me." he said. Almost without thought Jason struck the other boy.

Marcus struck back at him. The blow staggered Jason, but did not knock him down. Jason hit Marcus wildly. He drove at him a blow so hard that it took him off his feet. Marcus went down on the sand.

"Perhaps you will win at Elis," Jason cried, "but I have won here."

A heavy hand fell on Jason's shoulder. Jason looked to see the captain of the governor's guard. He was looking down at Marcus.

"Can you get up?" the soldier asked the Roman boy.

"Yes," the boy said, rising to his feet.

"Come with me," the soldier told Jason.

No one spoke until they had entered the governor's house and had come before the governor. Then, in quick words, the captain told the story of how he found Jason, the slave, beating the governor's son.

"Is that true?" the governor asked Jason.

"It is true."

"Why did you do this?" the governor asked.

Jason could not speak. His misery, his bitterness, and—although he would have denied it—his old affection for Marcus choked him.

"Why did you do this?" the governor repeated. Marcus stared at Jason. The soldier moved nearer. Still Jason said nothing.

"I am sorry," the governor said, "that I must punish you. You are a slave, Jason, but I have tried to treat you as the friend of my son. You have lost that friendship by what you have done. I must treat you now as any other slave. You shall go to work in the iron mines!"

The iron mines!

In them men worked night and day. In them men grew old and sick. In them men died. In them his own father had labored and died.

The work was cruelly hard. The work was slave's work. "I cannot do it, I cannot do it!" the boy's heart cried; but "You must do it!" his mind told him. With one last look at Marcus, a look filled with hate, Jason turned away, and followed the soldier from the governor's house.

His real slavery had begun.

II. THE IRON MINES

Often the boy Jason had seen the slaves on their way to and from the iron mines of Patmos. Never, until he was one of the sad procession, did he fully realize the misery of their lives.

Now Jason knew what it meant to labor from dawn to dusk and sometimes far into the night. Now he knew what it meant to be hungry, to be thirsty, to be hot, to be cold, to be sick without care, to grieve all the time.

In the shafts of the mines no one spoke but the slave-drivers. The slaves labored without speaking, without pause. Only when they came out of the mines and made their way to their miserable huts did they have any chance to speak with one another. Even then Jason had no desire to talk with his fellows. "Slaves!" he thought, despising them even more than he despised himself.

In the little time of daylight Jason sometimes had to himself he would go up on the cliff overlooking the beach where he had run with Marcus. From its rocks he would look down on the governor's house. One evening, as he watched, he saw Marcus come out. "I hate you," Jason flung at the other boy. "I shall never forgive you!"

Jason had thought himself alone, but to his surprise a voice sounded close to him. He turned around to see an old man standing near him. He had seen the man before, a slave going to and coming from the iron mines. He had never before been so close to him as he was now.

The man was, Jason thought, almost unbelievably old. Deep lines marked his thin face. Wrinkled skin stretched over his bony hands. It was his eyes, however, which caught and held the boy's gaze.

They were joyous eyes for a man so old. Dark and brilliant, they shone from hollow depths. They were eyes filled with love, friendly eyes, which even now cooled the anger of Jason.

"Why do you grieve?" the old man asked the boy.

"Because everyone is so cruel, so unfair to me," the boy cried.

"What has anyone done?"

As if his words were a river released from the holding of a dam Jason poured out his story. "I cannot enter the Olympian games, because I am a slave, and the only way I can win my freedom is by winning a race. They will keep me a slave forever!"

"No one can keep you a slave," the old man said, "if you want to be free."

"You are a slave," the boy exclaimed. "Can you make yourself free?"

"I am a slave under the Roman law," the old man said slowly. "I am no slave under the law of God. For, no matter how men drive my body, they cannot say what my soul shall do. Therefore I am free. You too shall be free. The Truth shall make you free. It is God's promise."

"Which God?" Jason demanded. "Apollo, who drives the heroes of the sun? Hermes, who is the messenger of all the gods? Zeus, who is the greatest of them all?"

"Not Apollo, not Hermes, not Zeus, not even the great Diana of the Ephesians," the old man said. "I speak of the one true God, the Alpha and Omega, the beginning and the end, the one almighty God."

"The one God?" Jason repeated. "Who is He? Where is He?"

"He is the Creator of heaven and earth, He is the earth, the sea, the sky. He is everywhere."

A call came then from one of the slave-drivers. The old man put his bony hand upon Jason's head. "May the peace of Almighty God be with you," he said and moved to go. "I shall see you again," he told Jason.

Through the days when he worked in the mines and the nights when he thought sadly over his misfortune, the boy often called to mind the old man's words. Who was this one God? Where was He? Not on Olympus, that high mountain of the old gods of Greece. The old gods had done nothing for men. They had not made them free. How had this old man found the one God?

The wonder grew in the boy until, at last, he sought out the old man. He found him, after the work of the day was done, seated near the door of a poor little hut. The old man was writing so busily that, for a time, he failed to see the boy. He was writing with a pointed reed and Egyptian ink upon a roll of papyrus. He put aside the roll and the reed when he saw Jason.

"Can I help you?" he asked the boy.

"Where can I find Him," Jason asked, "this one God of whom you have told me?"

"By His grace," the old man said, "God shows men the way to Him. He showed me the way through His only Son, our Lord and Savior Jesus Christ."

"You saw Him? The Son of God? You spoke with Him?" Jason's eyes grew wide. "How? Where? In a cloud? Upon a mountain?"

"I saw Him once upon a mountain, but He was not in a cloud. I knew Him as a Man. I lived with Him. I worked with Him. I went about with Him."

"You lived with Him? You worked with Him? What did He talk about?" Jason wanted to know.

"He taught us to love God, His Father, and to love one another."

The old man went back to his writing. In the fading light he set down the Greek letters upon the papyrus. Slowly Jason walked to his own hut. Who was this old man who knew Christ so well? What did the old man mean?

The questions stayed with the boy day after day, night after night. Freedom, the old man said, was something every man could win. God— the one God—gave it to the souls of men. Even when they were slaves, men could be free in their minds, in their thoughts. They could be free in body, as well as in mind, if only those who kept them in slavery would believe in Him and follow His command *Love one Another*. "Love one another," Jason thought. Did that mean that he had to love Marcus? "No, no!" he cried in anger.

Jason could not do that; but, little by little, he began to think of the other men and boys who worked in the mines. He began to see them as human beings like himself, grieving, sorrowing, hoping, fearing, loving, forgiving, seeking for something thay did not have. He began to wonder if the old man did not have the answer to all the questions that troubled them. *Love one Another*.

Would life be easier and better for all of them if they did?

The answer came closer to Jason when he was sent to the shaft where the old man was working. The slave-driver let him take his place beside the other slave, and even though they could not speak one with another while they worked, they became friends.

Sometimes Jason helped the old man at tasks which he thought beyond his strength. Sometimes the old man helped Jason with skills the boy did not have. In time they came to labor as a team.

After the work of the day was done, they often walked together toward the huts of the slaves. More than once Jason went back in thought to the Son of God, the Christ, whom the old man had known. "You saw Him? You heard Him?" he kept asking the old man.

"While He lived on earth I followed Him," the old man said. "I knew Him and loved Him."

"If Christ loves you, why are you a slave, left here to suffer?"

"Suffering for the love of God is not slavery," the old man said.

"It is not freedom," the boy insisted.

"To suffer for Christ wins eternal freedom," the old man told him.

"How can I find this freedom?"

"In God," the old man said.

"And how can I find Him?"

"Pray, my boy," the old man said. "Ask God to come to you. Ask

Him for the Light to see. He said, 'I am the Light.' "

The days dragged into weeks, and the weeks went from new moon to new moon. Jason still slaved in the iron mines of Patmos, while Marcus, the son of the governor, ran upon the sands of the Aegean shore, making ready for the footrace of the great Olympian games at Elis.

III. THE FREEMAN

The old man was ill. Jason missed him at the mines, and, when work was done, he went to the little hut. There was little he could do for his friend. He had no food to give him. He knew no way to help him. He could only bring him a drink of cool water from one of the island springs. The old man blessed him. "May God be with you, my son," he said.

"How shall I know God?" Jason asked himself, as he went up the rocks to the cliff. "How will He come to me?"

For a while the boy stared out over the sea, picturing again the sailing to the mainland of Greece of the boat which would take Marcus to the games. In a little while—perhaps tomorrow—the boat would go. He would not even see it, but he would know that Marcus had gone. Then, one day, Marcus would return. Would he wear the wreath of olive, the crown of the victor? "My crown," Jason thought sadly, and gazed toward the mainland, which he believed now that he should never see.

As Jason watched, he saw someone come out on the beach below. By his walk Jason knew him. Marcus! "I hate him." Jason started to say, then suddenly halted himself. He thought of the old man's words *love one another.* "I must not hate Marcus," he said slowly, "but I hope he cannot go to Elis."

From the height Jason kept watching the other boy. He saw Marcus plunge into the water and swim far out into the sea.

There had been a time when Jason would have leaped down from the rock, would have run across the sands, would have flung himself into the sea to swim with Marcus. In spite of their differences in rank Marcus had been his friend.

Now Jason could only watch him from the high cliff. Marcus, the son of the governor, was no longer friend of Jason, the slave of the mines.

After a time Jason saw Marcus turn back toward the shore. The Roman boy was not swimming easily. He was coming with difficulty. What was the trouble? Jason stood up as he heard a cry from the sea, a cry from Marcus, a cry for help.

For an instant Jason hesitated. What should he do? Marcus had taken from him the chance to win the race at Elis, but Marcus was calling for help. Marcus had taken from him the chance for glory, but Marcus needed him.

Jason thought of the old man's teaching. Quickly he made his decision. He would go to the boy who had been his friend. He would go to the boy he must love. With a shout he leaped down from the rock and ran across the beach. He could see Marcus struggling in the waves.

"Marcus, Marcus!" he shouted. "I am coming to you." Quickly he swam, stroke after stroke, until he came beside the drowning boy. He seized him and held him up. "Do not struggle with me," Jason said. "I am trying to save you. Let go, Marcus. I am taking you to shore."

Inch by inch, Jason made his way toward the beach. Of a sudden Marcus ceased struggling. Jason was tiring. Once he thought he could no longer hold Marcus. "O God," he prayed, "help me now, help us both!" He battled his way through the rough waters. Then, exhausted, Jason brought himself and the other boy upon the shore.

Arms reached out to them. Cries greeted them. "You have saved him," a voice praised him. Along the beach Jason heard the shouts, "Jason, the slave, has saved the son of the governor. Praise be to Jason!"

He turned toward Marcus. The boy's eyes were closed. "He lives?" Jason asked a man who was bending over the other boy.

"He lives," the man said.

"I am glad," said Jason.

A great cry went up along the shore as other men came running. A crowd gathered around the boys, but parted again as soldiers pushed them away with lifted spears. "The governor," someone said, and Jason struggled to his feet.

The governor lifted his son's head. "You are safe, Marcus," he told the boy.

"Jason saved me," Marcus said weakly.

"Jason?" The governor stared down at the slave boy. "You saved Marcus? After all you have said and done against him, against me? Why have you done this, Jason?"

"I cannot tell," the boy said, unable to say all that he felt. How could he tell men like these that he had saved Marcus because he loved him, and that he had prayed to God for help to love all men?

Marcus held out his hand to him. "I thank you, Jason," he said. His eyes told more than his words. "You will be my friend again?"

"I will be your friend," Jason promised.

The governor put his hand upon the shoulder of the slave. "Jason," he said, "I did you an injustice. I let you work with Marcus when I

92

knew that only freemen could enter the games. It was not fair to you. I will try now to do justice. From this day you are free, free to go with my son to Elis tomorrow."

"Free? Tomorrow?" Jason could say no more for joy.

"Tomorrow," said Marcus. "We shall sail together. Will you come with me now, Jason?"

"I will come back to you," Jason said. "I must go now and see someone who helped me."

Jason ran headlong through the crowd, not looking back. The crowd parted to let him pass. Men murmured words of praise to him, but he did not hear them. His one thought was to find the old man to tell him of his great happiness, to tell him how God's love had led him to save Marcus from the deep waters of the Aegean.

The old man was seated just outside the door of his hut. He was writing again with his reed pen and Egyptian ink upon the roll of papyrus. He did not see Jason as the boy drew near to him. He was so weary that the papyrus fell from his hand to the ground.

As the boy stopped to pick it up, he read the word at the top of the roll. It was the name of the writer. Jason did not know then or ever it was the name of an Evangelist, a name by which men would find the love of God through long ages. All he saw was one word in Greek. It read: JOHN

Being Different [4]

"There's a new girl in our class," Evin announced one Sunday at dinner. "Her name is Joyce Latimer, and she's adopted."

"That is interesting," her mother said. "But how do you happen to know she is adopted?"

"Miss Scott was showing lovely pictures of a Children's Home in New York City, and Joyce said she had spent most of her life in a Home like that. She said they had good food, and she liked having lots of children to play with. But . . . "

"Weren't the people who ran the place good to the children?"

"Yes, but she says none of that makes up for not having parents and a home of your own. She's so happy about being adopted. She says that, in addition to having such lovely parents and a nice room of her own and all, people are nicer to her now because she's not different any more."

"Why, how perfectly absurd!" exclaimed older sister Sally. "She

[4] By Ann Codrington. From *Trails for Juniors.* Copyright 1952 by Pierce & Smith. Used by permission.

was the same person she is now; why should they treat her any differently?"

"She didn't say people did horrid things to her; she meant they just didn't pay any attention to her, because they thought children from the Home didn't count—they were different."

"I recall Sally," Mrs. Holcomb said, smiling, "that once, when you were just Evin's age, you asked me how old people had to be before they began to want to be different. You were very serious about it, and evidently much troubled, but you never told me what it was."

"I'm sure your mother could have sympathized if you had told her, Sally," Mr. Holcomb said. "Do the children know about your third-grade experience, Jane?"

"No," Mrs. Holcomb said slowly. "Your father refers to the year when my mother taught in a mission school, just after your grandfather died. I think I have told you that she taught in a school for Negro children under the Board of Home Missions. But I never told you what an unhappy year it was for me. I went to the public school for white children. Naturally, I expected to make friends the first week. But I didn't. Weeks went by, and months went by, and nobody would play with me or even walk in line with me. I always had to walk alone at the end. At recess they would get off in groups and taunt me. I hadn't any idea what was wrong with me, and I couldn't ask Mother because I didn't want her to know. I think I was as wretchedly unhappy as a child could possibly be. When the children called me 'Nigger-lover' that should, I suppose, have given me a clue. But it didn't; I thought it was just a name. Finally, Mother found out about it, and she explained to me that there was nothing wrong with me at all— it was only because I had a mother who taught Negroes. And then Mother gave up her position, and we moved away. She began teaching in the college here, and—we lived happily ever after."

"But, even so, what a perfectly dreadful experience!" Sally gasped. "I'll bet you were the nicest, cutest little girl in that whole school! Those children missed a lot by not making friends with you," Evin added.

"You've said something there!" Peter declared. "And it's true of our nice Jewish doctor, too. People are missing a lot when they don't know him."

"Indeed they are," Mr. Holcomb agreed. "It is equally true of a Negro friend of mine. He's one of the finest men I ever met, but he surely has had a rough road to travel. That is often true—the people who are being snubbed are superior in intelligence and character to those who do the snubbing, and so the snubbers are cheating themselves. But, even when they don't happen to be very inter-

94

esting, there is no point in acting superior. However different they may be, people are—"

"—people," Peter chimed in.

"Thank you, Son. That's a perfect ending." And his father grinned companionably across at him.

There was a silence, and then Evin said, "Well, anyway, I'm glad Joyce got adopted. She's such a nice girl. But I wish I'd known her when she lived at the Home—I wouldn't have made her feel that she was different. Neither would Faith or Peggy."

"I believe that, Evie dear," Mr. Holcomb said. "Would that the world had more like you!"

Partners [5]

Danny Davis carefully climbed from his pony's back. He set his full jug safely on the ground. Not one drop had spilled. With two hands free he tied Beppo, his pony, to the post of the wire fence. Then he picked up the heavy jug and started across the fresh stubble of the wheat field.

The sun beat down upon the treeless plain. Grasshoppers jumped upon him with their feet like sticky pins. The sharp stubble pricked his bare feet, no matter how carefully he scuffed.

"I must teach Beppo to jump fences," thought Danny, "so that I won't have so far to walk."

He began to feel sorry for himself because of the hot walk he must take to carry the heavy jug of water to his father. Then he remembered how small was his part of the work compared with his father's. Here he came toward Danny now, bumping along on that noisy binder where he rode hour after hour under the hot sun. There was so much work to raising wheat from the time the ground was plowed until the golden grain was sold at the grain elevator.

That reminded Danny of the Chinese legend of the first wheat. It had seemed strange when he heard it at school; but now, out here in the wheat field, it seemed funnier than ever.

"Why the grin, Danny?" Mr. Davis stopped the horses beside Danny and climbed down from the binder.

Danny uncorked the jug and handed it to his father before answering. "I just remembered a Chinese legend we heard at school last year. I was thinking how little anyone must know about growing wheat to believe such a story."

---

[5] By Alice Geer Kelsey. Copyright 1939 by The Methodist Book Concern. Used by permission of the author.

"What is the legend, Danny, just the general idea of it?"

"Thousands and thousands of years ago, there was no wheat in the land. Finally someone did something that pleased God very much. They used a different name, but I suppose they meant God. He wanted to give this person a fine present and decided that wheat would be just the thing. So he sent him a present of wheat right straight from heaven. And that's how wheat came to the world."

"What's so funny about that?" Mr. Davis drained the jug.

"Why, Dad, when I think how you and the other farmers work to raise wheat, it makes me laugh to think of anyone saying that wheat could come as a present from God. Can you imagine it falling from the skies right into the grain elevator?" Danny looked out at the yellow fields that stretched as far as the eye could see. He looked at the gray cylinders far on the horizon, the grain elevators beside the railroad tracks. "And it's not just the work you farmers do with your plowing, planting, binding, threshing, and hauling to market. Think of the people who have worked in mines and factories and railroads so that you can have your machinery."

"You are right, son, that there are hours of work by many people behind every loaf of bread or dish of cereal that goes on our tables." Mr. Davis leaned on his binder and looked across the golden fields. "But, Danny boy, that is only part of the story."

Danny waited for his father to speak again. Instead, Mr. Davis began whistling a tune that sounded familiar, though Danny could not think where he had heard it. After whistling a bit, Mr. Davis began to sing the words:

> We plow the fields and scatter
> The good seed on the land,
> But it is fed and watered
> By God's almighty hand;
> He sends the snow in winter,
> The warmth to swell the grain,
> The breezes and the sunshine,
> And soft refreshing rain.

Then Danny remembered how the chorus went and joined his father:

> All good gifts around us
> Are sent from God above:
> Then thank the Lord, oh, thank the Lord
> For all his love.

Danny looked at his father, thinking, "I begin to see what those Chinese people meant."

"They had part of the truth," said his father, "and you had part of the truth."

96

"And that song we just sang," added Danny, "has all the truth. Farmers can work all day and all night plowing and planting, but it wouldn't do any good without God. He sends the rain and the sunshine. He puts in the ground the food that the seeds need. Inside of the seeds he puts whatever it is that makes them able to grow. When men and God work together, there is wheat to feed the world.

"It makes a farmer feel good to know that he and God are working together."

"Dad," said Danny, standing as tall as he possibly could. "I was nine years old last month. Isn't that old enough to start working on the wheat?"

Climbing back on the binder, Mr. Davis lifted Danny into his lap. Clucking to the horses, he pointed at a handle on the binder which Danny was to pull when his father called, "Now."

" It's good to work with God," said Danny.

And the father and son bumped round the great wheat field whistling. The words that went through their minds as they whistled were:

> We plow the fields and scatter
> The good seed on the land,
> But it is fed and watered
> By God's almighty hand.

I Never Thought Before [6]

What a day for a trip to Flatrock—the autumn air exciting, sun unexpectedly warm, the open road inviting! Eight boys, free from school, were jaunting this Saturday with Mr. Jones, their teacher from Bethel church school. Bareheaded, sweaters open and flapping, lunch bags swinging, these eleven-year-olds frisked along, free as colts turned out to pasture.

Jonathan and Stephen scuffed through the dried leaves and kicked them at each other in playfulness. Peter, new to the group, was trying to get Mr. Jones' attention. "How far is it to Flatrock? Will we eat as soon as we get there?" he asked.

"I imagine we'll be hungry enough by that two-hour climb."

Don's face wore a puzzled look. Stretching his stride to keep step with Mr. Jones, he looked ahead at Mike and Joe. The two boys were laughing boisterously and talking, in turn, as if they shared secrets. Joe, the smallest in the class, looked up confidently into Mike's face, and Mike glanced down on him almost as if Mike were a grownup.

[6] By Alberta Munkres. From *Trails for Juniors*. Copyright 1957 by The Methodist Publishing House. Used by permission.

Don knew what it was all about. Mike and Joe had been the day before to a "rabbit tease." At a neighbor's house, they had used sticks to prod the rabbits and scare them into jumping about the pen in a state of excitement. The more the boys prodded, the more scared the rabbits became. The more scared the rabbits grew, the more the boys laughed. Mike had told him all about it—even told him they were going again next Friday.

Don now glanced up at Mr. Jones with wonderment. "Does he know?"

Mr. Jones was laughing and talking, and paying no heed to the boys ahead.

Don's face relaxed. After all, this wasn't his problem. With that, he leaped out among the leaves, dropped his lunch bag, and began pelting Jonathan and Stephen with leaves until they sputtered and choked.

Unnoticed, Harry and Larry had lagged behind. Being twins, whatever one did, the other did also. Harry now turned out of his way to walk slowly and heavily over an anthill, remarking with a laugh, "I'll bet the little busybodies think I'm a Gulliver or something like that."

"I'll bet they don't now," remarked Larry dryly, as he gave a kick with his stout shoe, crashing in the top of the hill.

The group came together as they left the level road and took to the steep ascent. The boys slowed down with the strain of climbing. Now and again they stopped, puffed a bit, and pulled their sweater sleeves across their sweaty foreheads. The pace quickened for the last spurt of the climb and the group emerged onto Flatrock—the very top of the world, or so it seemed. Everywhere sky, sky, sky, like a vast overturned blue bowl; below, the river dark and solemn on its way to the sea; across the river, another high bank and on a tipmost projection, a gray stone house with bright red roof, perched as if ready for flight. The boys dropped down on the rock as if by common consent, opened their lunch bags. Little was heard save "ums" and "unhuhs" until the empty paper bags were blown up, popped, and cast into a park container.

Then the talking began. It all started when Jonathan leaned forward, pointed to the center of Flatrock, and whispered loudly, "Look!" There a little red creature made his way slowly on his six sturdy legs, staggering now and again under a burden almost his size.

"An ant!" cried Mike, crawling toward the traveler.

"Let's get him," came from Joe, at once on his hands and knees.

"We'll give him a good tease," retorted Mike, picking up a stick.

"Don't!" cried Jonathan. Then, like the little scientist that he was, added, "He's a worker. And he's taking that cookie crumb home to store for winter."

"Why don't you pick on something your own size," shouted Peter, his freckles showing brown against his flushed face.

Mike hesitated for a moment, then slowly let go of his stick and pushed

98

back to his place, pulling Joe with him. Shamefaced, he muttered, "I never thought before."

"Let's see where he goes," said Stephen, as if he had heard nothing.

The boys needed only to use their eyes, since just off the rock rose an anthill which the worker climbed slowly, then disappeared into its hole. Harry and Larry looked at each other, remembering a home they had destroyed.

"Smart little creatures!" Mr. Jones was saying. "They seem just to be running aimlessly here and there, but that isn't the case. Each has his special work to do—maids to milk the aphids, soldiers to bring home the conquered black ants, nurses for the baby ants, a queen for laying eggs and ruling the colony. If one is killed some other ant has to take over."

"I know something about the queen," said Jonathan. "If she is killed, that's nearly always the end of the colony."

Again Harry and Larry looked at each other. In each mind was the question, "Do you suppose I killed a queen?"

"Mr. Jones," said Stephen, "once I read a book about Dr. Schweitzer. It said he dosn't like to kill creatures. He has—what's the word?"

"Respect," supplied Mr. Jones, "or reverence, whichever you choose. It means that he wouldn't disturb creatures without thinking."

"Wouldn't he kill a mosquito?" grinned Peter, giving his arm a slap.

"Or a flea or a bee?" asked Mike.

"Or a gnat or a bat?" chimed in Joe.

"Would he step around a little old ant in his path?" asked Harry, and he and his brother laughed nervously.

Mr. Jones laughed at the fun, then spoke soberly, "This is the way I think it is. Dr. Schweitzer would never kill anything just for fun and he would never tease even the smallest creatures. But he would kill, if he thought he needed to do it, though he wouldn't like it even then."

"Would he kill ants?" ventured Larry.

"Yes, and I'll give you an example," answerd Mr. Jones. "When the traveler ants in Lambarene, Dr. Schweitzer's home, change locations they come marching by, five or six abreast. Once it took a column thirty-six hours to pass his house."

"Jeepers!" exclaimed the boys.

"They do not just pass by," continued Mr. Jones. "They destroy life. They even take bites out of people. So Dr. Schweitzer would have to do something to save the patients in his hospital and himself."

"But," added Mr. Jones, after the buzz of voices had died down, "when the ants march on, that ends it. He doesn't go after them and destroy them for fun."

"Would he kill termites?" asked Stephen. "Termites destroy a house if they get into the lumber."

"Yes," answered Mr. Jones. "He has to save his hospital."

"Would he kill a chicken to eat it?" inquired Peter. "Or is he—what do you call it?—a veg-e-tar-i-an?"

Everybody laughed and Mr. Jones had funny little wrinkles around his eyes. "Yes," he answered, "Dr. Schweitzer eats meat. He thinks that helps him to work and care for people in his hospital. He knows that life feeds on life—that is, some life is destroyed for the good of other life. Do you understand?"

"Yes," answered the boys.

"You mean," ventured Stephen, "like the spider we saw catch that fly?"

"Yes," answered Mr. Jones. "And a hungry frog might make a meal on the spider. Then if a man came along who wanted a dainty dish of frog's legs, that might be the end of the frog."

"But, changing the subject," said Mr. Jones, "what's the use of coming to Flatrock if we don't go exploring?"

"Whoopee!" shouted the boys and were up and away before Mr. Jones could so much as straighten out his legs. "Let's throw rocks into the river," cried one. "Let's climb that old tree and see what we can see."

When the boys got back, hot and panting, they dropped down on the rock again. "Peter and Don know some stories about Dr. Schweitzer and some of his pets," said Stephen. "Can't we hear them now?"

Mr. Jones nodded. "Who's first?"

Peter clasped his hands around his knees and began, "Once Dr. Schweitzer raised a fawn. He let him come into the house—right into the house, mind you! The fawn would lie down and listen while Dr. Schweitzer played his piano. And—funny thing!—one night the fawn got hungry and chewed up Dr. Schweitzer's own music."

"Ho, ho, ho!" laughed the boys.

Everybody now looked at Don, and Mike spoke for all when he said, "Go on, Don."

"Once Dr. Schweitzer had a pelican for a pet," began Don. "Dr. Schweitzer had cared for this bird since he was a baby. He gave him a home under his veranda and fed him until he was able to catch fish for himself. Once when his leg was broken, the doctor carried him each day to the river where he could fish and brought him home each night to safety."

"Go on," urged the boys.

"When the pelican grew up," Don continued, "he did not fly away with the other birds, but remained with his friend. Each evening at six o'clock when nearby mission bells rang, he would come from the river and perch on a high trellis gate to be Dr. Schweitzer's night watchman. And every morning at six o'clock when the bells rang again, he would fly away. But all night the doctor was safe. No one but himself and his helper might

100

come and go through the gate without a sharp rap on the head."

Laughter stopped the story and Don waited. Then he continued, "Whenever a guest came, Dr. Schweitzer would take him out and introduce him to the pelican. The great bird would flap his wings, thrust his long beak into the air, and make harsh noises in his throat."

"The guest's head would then be safe, eh?" laughed Mr. Jones.

"Well, boys," he continued, rising and stretching his legs, "time to be going! By the way, Miss Dean who has just returned from Lambarene is going to tell many things about the doctor and his way with animals, in the church-school building next Friday. Shall we go hear her?"

"Sure," came the answer.

Mike and Joe did not join the others. "Joe and I have something else to do," said Mike, looking not at Mr. Jones but down toward the river.

"Everybody has to decide for himself," said Mr. Jones, then added in friendly tone, "but if you change your minds. . . Come, fellows."

"Good-by, Flatrock!" said Peter.

"Good-by, ants!" cried Jonathan. "Get your work done before winter."

"Good-by, good-by!" called the boys.

When they got to level ground, Harry turned away to look at the ant hill he had disturbed. "Larry!" he called. "Come and look!"

Larry ran to the spot and what he saw caused him to give a long, low whistle. The ants, busy all day, had reopened the crown of their hill which he had kicked in, and were now going in and out as if nothing had happened.

"Some of them are dead, though," said Larry to himself, "and needn't be at all. But I guess the queen must still be alive." Then slowly he added, "I never thought before."

Mike and Joe hung behind. They were thinking and talking. They did not want to go with the kids next Friday, but . . . Just then a rabbit bounded across their path, a dog in hot pursuit. The rabbit looked wildly from side to side and leaped his long leaps with little hope of escape.

"Stop it!" cried Joe to the dog.

"Why don't you pick on something your size?" shouted Mike.

Dog and rabbit disappeared and the two boys stood looking at each other.

"I never thought . . ." said Joe.

"Well, you're not going to cry now, are you?" scolded Mike.

"I guess not," answered Joe, "but I'm not going to the rabbit tease."

"Well, who said I was?" answered Mike gruffly. "Come on!" The two boys quickened their pace and drew near the group at the outskirts of the village.

As the group broke up, the boys were saying to each other and to Mr. Jones, "Good-by! See you Friday!"

Mike called Don to one side, put his arm around his shoulder and whispered, "We'll come, Friday—both of us—Joe and I—you tell Mr. Jones."

What a day it had been at Flatrock for all the boys! Not one could ever again say, "I never thought before."

Woodland Neighbors [7]

The mink family had its den under the roots of a big hemlock tree on the shore of Pine Lake. It was a wonderful hiding place. Ted and Linda, the boy and girl who were spending the summer in a cabin near by, never suspected that the den was there.

But the children knew there were minks in the neighborhood. One morning, when they went for an early swim, they surprised Father Mink slipping along the stony beach with a big frog in his mouth. The frog was breakfast for the little ones in the den, but Ted and Linda did not guess that.

Before the mink whisked out of sight around a big rock, the children had time to see how handsome the long, graceful fellow was in his glossy coat of rich dark brown. It made them laugh, though, to see the funny way the mink ran. Because his body was so long and his legs so short, he humped up in the middle when he bounded through the woods.

"Like an inchworm," Linda chuckled.

"No worm ever moved as fast as that one," Ted protested, looking after the lithe, swift mink.

They searched in the ferns and juniper bushes near the big rock, hoping to find the entrance to the mink's den. There were plenty of chipmunk holes but not a sign of an opening large enough to admit a mink.

"I guess he just happened to be passing by here," Ted said at last.

Linda sighed. It would have been fun to hide in the bushes and watch the minks, to study their ways. A few mornings later Ted and Linda were in the rowboat, floating quietly near shore in the green shadow of the pines and hemlocks that lined the bank. Suddenly they saw a dark animal swimming with its head and sleek back quite high in the water.

"It's another mink," Ted whispered.

Linda stared at the animal, blinked her eyes, and looked again. "Oh, Ted!" she breathed. "There's a little one riding on the big one's back."

Ted grinned delightedly. "I see him. The little booger looks like he's having a wonderful time."

Mother Mink swam quickly out of sight around a point of land and

[7] By Virginia Frances Voight. From *Trails for Juniors.* Copyright 1957 by The Methodist Publishing House. Used by permission.

the children could not see her go ashore near the big hemlock.

Mother or Father Mink would often take one or another of their little ones for packaback rides along the lake shore. The little minks couldn't swim very well yet, but they had swimming lessons every day. Before the summer was over they would be almost as much at home in the water as the fish themselves.

There were five furry little minks in the hemlock den. They had been born almost two months before, not much bigger than peanuts, and with their eyes closed. Now they had grown fat and saucy and their keen eyes sparkled like tiny jewels. There were lively times under the hemlock roots when the youngsters commenced their rough play. They would cuff one another, bite, roll over and over, and chase their mother's bushy tail. All to the tune of baby snarls, growls and squeaks.

When one of their parents was there to watch them, the little minks were allowed to romp on the beach before the den. There were many interesting things to do on the beach. There were crawfish to be poked out from underneath the stones, and minnows to be caught in the shallow water among the stems of arrowhead and pickerel weed. At dusk it was fun to watch the gnats and mosquitoes dance above the lake, and to chase the lively hoptoads that splashed in and out of the water. Sometimes big moths would drift above the beach on down-soft wings. The baby minks would spring into the air to try to catch them, but usually the moths floated easily out of reach.

Life wasn't all play for the mink family. Often danger threatened from the air and from the forest behind the den.

When the hunting cry of the Great Horned Owl boomed through the twilight, Mother Mink would bark a warning for her children to run to the den. There is nothing that an owl would rather have for supper than a young mink.

Sometimes Brownie, the littlest mink, wouldn't heed a warning quickly enough. Then Mother Mink would flash out and catch him by the scruff of his neck with her sharp teeth, and run back to the den with him. Safe inside, she'd give him a sharp cuff with her paw. In this way she taught the little ones that an owl is greatly to be feared.

The red fox, with his crafty ways, and the soft-footed bobcat, who could steal through the pine gloom as silently as a shadow, were other neighbors to be mistrusted.

On the other hand, squirrels, chipmunks, wood mice, and rabbits all feared the hunting minks.

One day Mother Mink decided it was time the children had a real workout in swimming. Until now all they had done was to paddle about in the shallows near the den. This time Mother Mink whined softly for them to follow as she headed out around the wooded point.

Ted and Linda were fishing that morning. Their rowboat was anchored just around the point from the hemlock den. Linda was sitting on the stern seat and Ted was amidships. They hadn't yet had time to get their fishlines in the water when Mother Mink appeared, all five little minks dog-paddling bravely behind her.

Ted sucked in his breath. "Look!" he whispered.

Linda nodded. Her eyes were very wide as she watched the oncoming minks.

The children sat so still that Mother Mink probably thought the boat was a rock. Ted saw that she was going to pass very close to them. He reached down a stealthy hand and gripped the long handle of his fishing net. He just had to capture one of those baby minks for a pet!

He let Mother Mink and four of the little minks swim past. Brownie Mink was the last in line. He was trying hard to keep up with his family, but his legs were shorter than those of the others and couldn't paddle as fast. When this little lone one came opposite the boat, Ted swooped down with the long-handled net. Suddenly Brownie found himself tangled in the meshes and being lifted into the air. He sent a squeal of terror after his mother.

Up ahead, Mother Mink's sharp ears heard the call for help. Warning her other children to wait right where they were she swam hastily back to see what had happened to Brownie.

Ted hoisted the net into the boat and set it down gently between him and Linda. They could see the fat little mink squirming helplessly in the wet meshes. He was badly scared, but he was angry, too. He kept squealing and squeaking with rage.

"Isn't he cute!" Linda bent down for a better look. She poked a finger playfully against the net, Brownie growled and tried to nip her.

Neither Ted nor Linda noticed Mother Mink swimming toward the boat. But suddenly they heard an angry hissing and caught a whiff of strong, musky odor, such as minks give out when they are upset.

"What's that awful smell?" Linda asked, wrinkling her nose.

Ted didn't have to answer because just then Mother Mink scrambled over the side of the boat. She clung to the gunwale, hissing and showing her sharp teeth. Her eyes glittered dangerously.

"Jeepers," Ted muttered. "She's trying to decide which of us to go for first."

He had heard an old guide tell his father that a mink was a fearless fighter. And he had been warned that all wild mothers will fight to protect their little ones.

Linda edged to the far side of the stern seat. "She—she wants her baby back," she faltered.

Ted hesitated. He hated to give up his wild pet. What should he do?

Just then Brownie squeaked again. Mother Mink darted furiously at the net. Hastily Ted grabbed the net and turned it upside down over the side of the boat.

Brownie splashed into the water and sank. His mother promptly dove in after him. In a moment they both bobbed up, Mother Mink holding Brownie by the scuff of his neck. Brownie pawed at his mother and struggled up on her back. She swam away to where the four other little minks were floating, all in a row. Brownie slipped into the water and took his place at the end of the line.

The mink family paddled back around the point, headed for home.

Linda looked after them with a sigh. "I guess a baby mink wouldn't make a very good-natured pet," she said wistfully.

Ted nodded. "I'll keep my landing net for fish after this," he decided.

Flying Wedge [8]

Duncan looked at the lowered head of his friend, bent over the checker-board, trying to figure out the next move. Tim was so white-looking and thin, it was hard now to imagine him hitting a home run or winning a foot race, and yet not so long ago he had been able to do both those things. Duncan felt a tiny surge of impatience inside as he wondered how much longer it would be before Tim could stop these everlasting checker games and run with the gang once more.

Tim moved his checker, then looked up and caught Duncan's glance. "Willikers, Dunc, you've no idea how good it feels to get out of bed! Those three months seemed like three years!"

"They did to me, too," Dunc agreed, thinking of all the afternoons he had reluctantly left the gang to come keep Tim company.

"I appreciate your spending so much time with me. I know you'd have had more fun with the others."

"Aw, that's okay." Dunc lowered his head and was busy deciding where to move his checker. He was suddenly ashamed of the number of times his mother had had to remind him that Tim was lonesome. "Did you ask the doctor whether you can go to the Wheeler ranch to hunt arrowheads with our boys' club Saturday?"

Tim's eyes shone. "He said I could! Of course, I'm not allowed to walk around much. But just getting outside again will be wonderful!"

Dunc looked at his watch. "I'd better get going. I told Mom I'd be home early. See you Saturday!"

Outside, he stood for a moment breathing deeply in the crisp air and

[8] By Dorothy Dill Mason. From *Trails for Juniors.* Copyright 1955 by Pierce and Washabaugh. Used by permission.

enjoying the feel of his own healthy body. Suddenly the crack of a bat hitting a ball came to Dunc's ears. "There goes a homer!" he told himself, and ran swiftly to the vacant lot.

Saturday was a beautiful day, sunny but not too warm. When the car stopped for Tim, he was out on the porch. As he came down the walk, the boys all cheered. Excitement had given Tim's thin cheeks bright spots of color, and as the boys pounded him on the back in greeting, the spots grew even brighter. "Welcome back, Tim," said Mr. Hardy, the club leader, smiling over his shoulder.

"Now that we're all together again, we'll have a real day," announced Jack in his hearty way.

"Chet, Bimbo, Jack, Dunc, and Tim!" chanted Dunc. "The Five Fearless Fellows!"

"Fond of Fighting Fires and Freeing Frantic Folks From Fixes!" added Tim.

"Full of Fun and Frolic!" shouted Chet.

"Also Full of Foolishness!" Mr. Hardy grinned.

The Wheeler ranch was thirty miles out of town, so the boys had plenty of time for both fun and foolishness before they arrived. Mr. Wheeler met them at the ranch gate with the news. "I should have told you to come sooner. The geese left yesterday."

"Geese?" Mr. Hardy asked. "What geese?"

"They stop every year at our big pond on their way north." Mr. Wheeler said. "Musta been most a hundred. A few days ago they started leavin', about twenty-five at a time. Only three left now."

"Three? Why didn't they go?" Jack asked.

Mr. Wheeler scratched his head. "Maybe you fellers would like to run over in the car and see for yourselves. Pond's about a quarter of a mile along this road," he explained to Mr. Hardy, and he squeezed into the front seat.

The three geese were over at the far end of the big pond. Mr. Wheeler pointed out the middle one. "He musta hurt his wing during the stop-over," he explained. "Anyway, when the last of the crowd left yesterday, he tried to go along, but he couldn't get off the water."

"Where did the other two come from?" Chet asked.

"I'm comin' to that," Mr. Wheeler said. "Well, sir, those fellers all got up in the air in formation, the way they do. Then they musta looked down and seen this cripple. Would you believe it, the last two peeled off like a coupla fightin' planes and dived right back to the pond again. One got on each side of—Look! There they go now."

While the boys watched, the three big geese lined up at one edge of the pool. Along the surface of the water they skittered, wings flapping getting ready to take off. The two outside ones pulled up off the pond.

106

The middle one couldn't get into the air. The two flew around for a moment and dropped back to the pond again.

"They've been doing that all day," Mr. Wheeler said. "Time and time again."

"They're trying to help the cripple fly," Tim breathed softly.

"Will they stay with him all summer?" Dunc asked.

Mr. Wheeler shook his head. "Probably not. They will leave with the next wedge that comes along. Their instinct will make 'em go." He turned toward the car. "Get your gear and picnic lunches," he told the boys. "We'll start hiking from here."

"How far is it to where we look for arrowheads?"

"It's a three-mile hike to the old dry lake bed. It's the best spot around. The Indians used to shoot the geese that stopped there. Every time they missed, they lost an arrow into the water. Some of them they retrieved, but a lot they lost."

"Three miles," Mr. Hardy looked thoughtfully at Tim, who pretended to be studying the crippled goose.

Mr. Wheeler chuckled. "Ye're not a bunch of tenderfeet, are ye? That's not so far from here!"

"No," Mr. Hardy agreed, "but one boy—"

"That's all right." Tim spoke up quickly. "You fellows go on. I'll wait here."

Dunc stared at Tim, who avoided his eyes. Dunc had been looking forward to this trip for a month. He had a small arrowhead collection, and it wasn't often he got a chance to add to it. He just had to go with the others. He was tired of always keeping Tim company. Tim would be all right alone.

"I don't think—" Mr. Hardy began.

"Listen!" Chet exclaimed. Everyone froze in his tracks. From far, far above came a faint wild sound. Etched against the blue sky was a large wedge of wild geese, moving fast. They were so high up they were only black dots on the blue.

With excited honkings the geese on the pond lined up once more. Again they taxied across the surface for a take-off. Again the outside two rose into the air, while the cripple tried in vain. This time the others didn't return. Their powerful, healthy wings pushed hard as they hurried after their distant brothers.

Dunc found himself staring at Tim again. Tim was looking at the crippled goose, now slowly and sadly paddling back alone. "Never mind, fella," Tim said in a low voice. "They'll come back for you someday. At least—I think—they will."

Suddenly Dunc hated the deserting geese. How could they go off and leave a wounded comrade? But then his common sense reminded him that, like other creatures, they lived by instinct. In their short stay with their crippled brother they had already done more than could be expected of them. But man—now man was different. God has given man the capacity for love. Love for his fellow man was what raised human beings above all other living creatures.

Dunc suddenly turned to Jack. "While you're looking, find a couple of extra arrowheads for Tim and me, will you?"

Jack clapped him on the back, "I sure will!"

"We'll divide up all we find," Chet added.

Tim gave Dunc a level look. "You don't need to stay." He added in a lower tone, "Please don't feel sorry for me. I'm all right."

"Who's feeling sorry for you?" Dunc exclaimed. "I was just thinking what a good chance to get some specimens here at the pond for our nature study class."

"You can use the rowboat," Mr. Wheeler said. "It's over beyond those rushes."

"Thanks!" Dunc's voice was enthusiastic, now.

Tim's face relaxed, and the guarded look went out of his eyes. As the others left, Tim turned toward the boat. Dunc hung behind for a moment. "Just be patient," he whispered to the drifting goose. "They'll be back. I *know* they will."

"Dear UNICEF" [9]

The juniors had just received a gift. It was a beautiful big flag of the United Nations. They had a little one they had made, but this was something quite different. Sarah Pierce's father had given it to them. "Shouldn't we have a program on the United Nations to sort of dedicate it?" Bond asked their superintendent.

"Indeed we should, Bond," Mrs. Morgan agreed. "And what would you think about asking Sarah to give a talk?" That met with immediate and wholehearted approval.

"Sarah's so quiet," Bond said. "She knows such a lot, but she never brags about anything. We never knew until she brought the flag this morning that she has been at the United Nations building. Three different times she has gone with her father. Boy, that must have been something!"

Sarah consented to talk at the assembly period the following Sunday morning.

"Because there is so much to tell about the United Nations," she began,

[9] By Ann Codrington. From *Trails for Juniors.* Copyright 1953, by Pierce and Washabaugh. Used by permission.

"I decided to talk about just one branch of it. The part that interests me most is the UNICEF. You know what that stands for, I guess." Seeing only a few heads nod, she explained, "It means United Nations International Children's Emergency Fund.

"When this committee was appointed, six years ago last December, there wasn't a cent to work with. There wasn't anything else to work with, either, and yet they started out to help all of the needy children of the world. The people of Norway raised money by having each one give a day's wages, and then people in other countries began doing the same thing. That gave the committee something to start with. The next year our United States gave money, from the government, and then many other governments decided to do that, too. Now, fifty-eight governments have given money for the children, and it adds up to $117,000,000."

"Whe-e-w-w!" came from some of the juniors.

Sarah smiled and said, "That is a lot of money, isn't it? But there are 900,000,000 children in the world. Some of us are fortunate enough not to need help from UNICEF, but there are millions and millions of children who do."

She went on to explain how the money has been used—to feed children, to clean them up, to clothe them, and to doctor them. And then she said, "I don't want to tell you things you already know. Won't you ask questions? I may not be able to answer them, but I will try."

Philip's hand went up. "I think you said UNICEF had helped children in seventy countries. Aren't there just sixty countries in the United Nations?"

"Yes, that is right. But the work of UNICEF is to help *all* children in need, whether their countries are members of the United Nations or not."

Bruce had a question. "You said fifty-eight countries gave the money; but where did all the food and clothing come from?"

"From every country that could furnish it. One of the things our country has furnished is milk—powdered milk, of course. Some had meat to share, some had sugar, some had wheat, some had cod-liver oil or shark-liver oil. Some countries helped by furnishing labor. For example, our cotton was sent to Japan and made into cloth, and then into garments for children in Korea. Guatemala had coffee, but since coffee is not good for children, it was sold in New York and the money was used to buy milk."

"Oh, I see. Thank you."

A fifth-grade girl asked, "Is it true that children from other countries send doll clothes to the United Nations? Somebody said they did."

"Oh, yes. Children from all over the world write thank-you letters. They start their letters 'Dear UNICEF.' Often they send little gifts to show how grateful they are. Sometimes they send pictures, or small flags of their countries, or little dolls they have dressed, or maybe just doll clothes they have made. Usually they end their letters with 'Long Live the United Nations!'"

"I've often heard people criticize the United Nations," Bond said. "I guess we people who aren't hungry and cold and sick just don't appreciate it. Probably we notice its mistakes and overlook the good it does."

"Yes, that is true," Sarah said. "My father thinks, though, that our indifference is even worse than our criticisms. So many people just are not interested."

"Is there anything we can do about that?" Prudence asked. "If we raised some money, by going without ice cream and candy, it wouldn't be enough to do any good, would it?"

"Yes, Prudence, it would. I *hoped* somebody would ask about that, and so I wrote this down." Sarah picked up a poster and put it where everyone could see. On it she had written six different ways in which a dollar can help. In each of the six spaces she had fastened a real dollar bill.

"My grandmother gave me these six dollars," she explained. "She thought it would be a beginning, in case you wanted to raise some money. She said if you didn't, I could add whatever I saved and then send it in." Sensing the eagerness in the group, Sarah asked, "Oh, do you really want to? That would be lovely!"

Bond stood up and said, "All you who want to raise money for UNICEF put up your hands."

And every hand in the room went up.

BOOKS[1]

GENERAL BOOKS ON CAMPING

Bogardus, LaDonna. *The Church Day Camp.* National Council of the Churches of Christ in the U.S.A. 60 cents.

Bogardus, LaDonna. *Planning the Church Camp for Juniors.* National Council of the Churches of Christ in the U.S.A. $1.00.

Hammett, Catherine Tilley. *Campcraft ABC's for Camp Counselors.* Girl Scouts of the U.S.A. $1.25.

Mitchell, A. Viola and Crawford, Ida B. *Camp Counseling.* Philadelphia: W. B. Saunders Co., 1950. $4.75.

CAMPCRAFT

Hammett, Catherine Tilley. *Your Own Book of Campcraft.* New York: Pocket Books, Inc., 1946. 35 cents.

Hammett, Catherine Tilley. *Campcraft ABC's for Camp Counselors.* Girl Scouts of the U.S.A. $1.25.

Nothing's More Fun Than Eating Outdoors. National Dairy Council. Chicago. 10 cents for 1-100 copies.

NATURE CRAFTS

Jaeger, Ellsworth. *Easy Crafts.* New York: Macmillan Co., 1947. $2.49.

Price, Betty. *Adventuring in Nature.* New York: National Recreation Association, 1939. $1.25.

Stinson, Thelma. *Native 'N' Creative.* No. 9500-BC. Nashville. Board of Education of The Methodist Church. 40 cents.

FOR BOTH CAMPERS AND COUNSELORS

Basic Science Education Series. Row, Peterson & Co., Evanston, Illinois.

> *Balance in Nature.* 52 cents.
> *Beyond the Solar System.* 52 cents.
> *Birds.* 48 cents.
> *The Earth a Great Storehouse.* 48 cents.
> *The Earth's Nearest Neighbor.* 52 cents.
> *Foods.* 52 cents.
> *Insects and Their Ways.* 48 cents.

---

[1] Prices subject to change without notice. May be secured from your denominational publishing house.

Living Things. 48 cents.

Plant and Animal Partnership. 48 cents.

Plant Factories. 48 cents.

The Sky Above Us. 48 cents.

Stories Read from the Rocks. 48 cents.

The Sun and Its Family. 52 cents.

Toads and Frogs. 48 cents.

Trees. 48 cents.

You as a Machine. 48 cents.

Bird Houses and Feeders. National Audubon Society. 15 cents.

Homes for Birds. Superintendent of Documents. Washington, D. C., 15 cents.

The World We Live In. Editorial Staff of *Life* and Lincoln Barnett. New York: Simon and Schuster, 1956. $4.95.

Bartlett, Ruth. *Insect Engineers.* New York: William Morrow and Company, 1957. $2.75.

Beck, Helen L. *Going to Camp.* New York: Fred Ungar Publishing Co., 1950. $1.95.

Buck, Margaret Waring. *In Woods and Fields.* New York and Nashville: Abingdon Press, 1950. Cloth, $3.00; paper, $1.75.

Buck, Margaret Waring. *In Ponds and Streams.* Nashville: Abingdon Press, 1955. Cloth, $3.00; paper, $1.75.

Buck, Margaret Waring. *Pets from the Pond.* New York and Nashville, Abingdon Press. 1958. Cloth, $3.00; paper, $1.75.

Cormack, Maribelle. *The First Book of Stones.* New York: Franklin Watts, Inc., 1950. $1.95.

Cormack, Maribelle. *The First Book of Trees.* New York: Franklin Watts, Inc., 1951. $1.95.

Dickinson, Alice. *The First Book of Plants.* New York: Franklin Watts, Inc., 1953. $1.95.

Evans, Eva Knox. *All About Us.* New York: Simon and Schuster. 1947. $2.50.

Fenton, Carroll Lane and Pallas, Dorothy Constance. *Trees and Their World.* New York: The John Day Company, 1957. $3.25.

Fenton, Carroll Lane and Pallas, Dorothy Constance. *Insects and Their World.* New York: The John Day Company, 1956. $2.95.

Fenton, Carroll Lane and Fenton, Mildred Adams. *Our Changing Weather.* Garden City, New York: Doubleday and Company, Inc., 1954. $2.50.

Fenton, Carroll Lane and Fenton, Mildred Adams. *Rocks and Their Stories.* Garden City, New York: Doubleday and Company, Inc., 1951. $2.75.

Garland, Joseph. *All Creatures Here Below.* Boston: Houghton Mifflin Co., 1954. $2.00.

Hogner, Dorothy Childs. *Frogs and Polliwogs.* New York: Thomas Y. Crowell Co., 1956. $2.50.

Hogner, Dorothy Childs. *Spiders.* New York: Thomas Y. Crowell Co., 1955. $2.50.

Lathrop, Dorothy P. *Let Them Live.* New York: Macmillan Co., 1951. $2.75.

Peattie, Donald Culross. *The Rainbow Book of Nature*. New York: The World Publishing Company, 1957. $4.95.

Peterson, Roger T. *A Field Guide to the Birds*. Boston: Houghton Mifflin Co., 1947. $3.95.

Wherry, Edgar T. *Wild Flower Guide*. New York: Doubleday & Co., 1948. $3.95.

Zim, Herbert S. *Frogs and Toads*. New York: William Morrow and Company, 1950. $2.50.

Zim, Herbert S. *Lightning and Thunder*. New York: William Morrow and Company, 1952. $2.50.

Zim, Herbert S. *Owls*. New York: William Morrow and Company, 1950. $2.50.

Zim, Herbert S. *Rabbits*. New York: William Morrow and Company, 1948. $2.50.

Zim, Herbert S. *Snakes*. New York: William Morrow and Company, 1949. $2.50.

Zim, Herbert S. *The Sun*. New York: William Morrow and Company, 1953. $2.50.

STORYBOOKS

Brown, Jeanette Perkins. *The Storyteller in Religious Education*, with an appendix of stories for telling. Boston: Pilgrim Press, 1951. $2.00.

Hazeltine, Alice I., Comp. *Children's Stories to Read and Tell*. New York and Nashville: Abingdon Press, 1949. $2.50.

Kelsey, Alice Geer. *The Teakwood Pulpit and Other Stories for Junior Worship*. New York and Nashville: Abingdon Press, 1950. $1.75.

HYMNBOOKS AND SONGBOOKS

Fun and Folk Songs. Rev. ed. Philadelphia: Westminster Press. 25 cents.

Hymns for Junior Worship. Philadelphia: Westminster Press, 1940. $1.50.

Sing a Tune. Cooperative Recreation Service, Delaware, Ohio. 25 cents.

Thomas, Edith Lovell, ed. *Singing Worship*. New York and Nashville: Abingdon Press, 1935. $1.75.

Thomas, Edith Lovell, ed. *The Whole World Singing*. New York: Friendship Press, 1950. Cloth, $2.95; paper, $1.95.

RECREATION

Games for Quiet Hours and Small Spaces. New York: National Recreation Association, 1938. 75 cents.

Harbin, E. O. *Games for Boys and Girls*. New York and Nashville: Abingdon Press, 1951. Cloth, $2.00; paper, $1.35.

Hunt, Sarah, and Cain, Ethel. *Games the World Around*. New York: Ronald Press. $4.00.

Millen, Nina. *Children's Games from Many Lands*. New York: Friendship Press, 1943. Cloth, $2.95; paper, $1.95.

MUSIC [2]

Grand Canyon Suite. Victor Album LM1928. $4.95.
Overture to William Tell. Victor Album LM1986. $4.95.
Prelude Op. 28, No. 15, by Chopin. Victor Album LM1168. $4.95.

---

[2] Prices subject to change without notice. Secure from your local record store.

NOTES

NOTES

NOTES

NOTES